"Teachers of all levels can use these suggestions
to create interest and lighten the atmosphere."
—*Infotech*

"Studies have shown that humor helps to get kids' attention,
makes them retain more, reduces stress, and makes the school day fly by—
something that's good for students and teachers. So, lighten up!"
—*Educational Dealer*

LAUGHING LESSONS

149⅔ WAYS
to Make Teaching and Learning Fun

BY RON BURGESS

Edited by Cynthia Nelson and Darsi Dreyer

free spirit
PUBLiSHiNG®

Helping kids
help themselves™
since 1983

Library of Congress Cataloging-in-Publication Data

Burgess, Ron.
    Laughing lessons : 149 2/3 ways to make teaching and learning fun / by Ron Burgess.
        p.   cm.
    Includes bibliographical references and index.
    ISBN 1-57542-075-9
        1. Teaching. 2. Humor in education. I. Title.

    LB1027 .B82 2000
    371.102—dc21

                                                                                    99-056599

At the time of this book's publication, all facts and figures cited are the most current available; all telephone numbers, addresses, and Web site URLs are accurate and active; all publications, organizations, Web sites, and other resources exist as described in this book; and all have been verified as of February 2004. The author and Free Spirit Publishing make no warranty or guarantee concerning the information and materials given out by organizations or content found at Web sites, and we are not responsible for any changes that occur after this book's publication. If you find an error or believe that a resource listed here is not as described, please contact Free Spirit Publishing. Parents, teachers, and other adults: We strongly urge you to monitor children's use of the Internet.

The "Make a Fold-Out Book" activity on page 105 is adapted from *Growing Good Kids: 28 Activities to Enhance Self-Awareness, Compassion, and Leadership* by Deb Delisle and Jim Delisle, Ph.D. (Minneapolis: Free Spirit Publishing, 1996), and is used with permission.

Permission is granted for individual readers, teachers, and group leaders to photocopy the pages included in the "List of Reproducible Pages" (page vi) for personal, classroom, or group work only. Photocopying or other reproduction of these materials for an entire school or school system is strictly prohibited.

Cover design: Percolator
Book design and layout: Percolator
Illustrations: Marieka Heinlen
Index: Kay Schlembach

14   13   12   11   10   9   8   7   6   5
Printed in the United States of America

Free Spirit Publishing Inc.
217 Fifth Avenue North, Suite 200
Minneapolis, MN 55401-1299
(612) 338-2068
help4kids@freespirit.com
www.freespirit.com

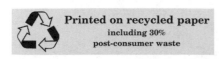

Printed on recycled paper
including 30%
post-consumer waste

Dedication

This book is dedicated to Louise-Sandy, my best friend and wife.
For all the years of laughing, loving, and living.
Always and forever.

AND

To Lisa Anderson, a very good friend,
who helped me dot all the t's and cross all the i's and laughed at my jokes.

Acknowledgments

I would like to acknowledge Launa Ellison, Linda Nason McElherne, and
Cynthia Nelson for their contributions to the development of *Laughing Lessons*.

And thank you to the staff at Free Spirit Publishing including Darsi Dreyer,
Jessica Thoreson, Marjorie Lisovskis, and Judy Galbraith.

Contents

List of Reproducible Pages

Introduction

"He who laughs most, learns best."
—John Cleese

Laughing Lessons? What does laughter have to do with teaching anyway? How does humor apply to you and your classroom? Why should you add something else to your already jam-packed curriculum? Let me try to explain why I believe laughter and humor are important to you and the kids you teach, and what I'd like this book to do for you.

I wrote it to:

★ help you see the importance of a pleasant, good-humored environment
★ convince you that laughter can be an essential element in learning
★ help you use the fun that already exists in your classroom
★ bring more joy into your teaching
★ show you ways to combine laughter with learning.

The dictionary defines humor as "the ability to perceive, enjoy, or express what is funny or comical." Everyone has one or more of these abilities. We use our sense of humor when we enjoy a joke, read a humorous story, or watch a funny TV show or movie. We can also use it when we teach. Even if you don't think you're particularly funny, you can get kids to laugh. Children love to laugh. It seems at times they'll laugh at anything. As teachers we can capitalize on this humor and laughter and use it to our advantage.

Psychologists, psychiatrists, and researchers have written that humor can be a positive force in teaching, learning, and health. Developmental psychologist Paul E. McGhee has researched the role of humor in the classroom. His studies have shown, among other things, that young students learn better when lessons are presented with humor. Their recall improves when tests use humorous examples, and the material is retained up to one month longer.[1] According to brain researcher and author Candace B. Pert, "Positive emotional experiences are much more likely to be recalled when we're in an upbeat mood, while negative emotional experiences are recalled more easily when we're already in a bad mood. Not only is memory affected by the mood we're in, but so is actual performance."[2] There is a direct connection between a pleasant experience and better memory. In *The Schools Our Children Deserve,* Alfie Kohn writes that high achievement is a by-product of interest: "Where interest appears, achievement usually follows."[3] The brain is designed to scan for novelty. Thus, by creating a happy, interesting, stimulating, and laughing classroom we help promote better learning.

Humor doesn't just help the kids. A study by Richard Weaver and Howard Cotrell concluded that humor helps teachers reveal a comfortable, secure attitude about themselves, the material they are teaching, and their relationship with their students.[4] And William Fry, a Stanford University psychiatrist, points out that laughter is an excellent workout for the body. It improves blood pressure, stimulates circulation, boosts the immune system, raises endorphin levels, exercises the lungs, and benefits the heart and respiratory system. In addition, he says, laughter and positive emotions produce beneficial chemical changes in the body, changes that aid healing in people who are ill.[5]

These and other studies prove that humor and laughter can be helpful in the classroom. Laughter and humor will hold kids' attention, thus helping them retain the information they're learning. Humor also helps reduce tension, both mental and physical, in the kids *and* you. Laughter is a great stress reliever. It can make the school day seem shorter and your load lighter. It can help you cope with crisis, break monotony, and live longer. Job relief and health benefits. What more could you ask for? He—or she—who laughs...lasts.

This book is about humor—it's not a humor book. There aren't any lists of jokes. It's not a how-to book or a step-by-step guide for using humor. It's a collection of humor-filled ideas that have worked for me and for other teachers in the classroom. You could call it

---

1 McGhee, Paul E., *Children's Humour* (New York: J. Wiley, 1980) and *Humor and Children's Development: A Guide to Practical Applications* (Binghamton, NY: Haworth Press, 1989).

2 Pert, Candace B., *Molecules of Emotion: Why You Feel the Way You Feel* (New York: Scribner, 1997), p. 144.

3 Kohn, Alfie, *The Schools Our Children Deserve* (New York: Houghton Mifflin, 1999), p. 128.

4 Weaver, Richard, and Howard Cotrell, "Ten Specific Techniques for Developing Humor in the Classroom," in *Educational Journal*, vol. 108, no. 2, p. 167–179.

5 Fry, William, *Sweet Madness: A Study of Humor* (Palo Alto, CA: Pacific Books, 1970).

a treasury of suggestions and ideas. Dip in wherever you wish. Start at the end, at the beginning, or in the middle. The ideas are yours to use, refine, work on, expand, enlarge, combine, or juggle around in any way you see fit.

I can't promise that this book will turn you into a stand-up comic, get you a weekly TV series, or even get you elected teacher of the year. That's not its purpose. What I *can* promise is that the book's suggestions for injecting humor into your teaching will increase your effectiveness, make the curriculum come alive, enhance children's creativity, and encourage skill development. As you read along, you'll probably think of additional ideas that you have used, other areas where you could use humor, and more ways to reuse some of this material. Once you get started, ideas will start to flow.

You can't give a smile away—people always give it back. I'd like it if *you'd* send a smile my way and let me know how *Laughing Lessons* works for you. What ideas did you try? Which ones were most successful in your classroom? What were you most comfortable doing? What made you and your students laugh out loud? If you came up with a great new idea, or if you modified or changed a suggestion and it made the kids roll with laughter, please tell me about it. Here's where you can reach me:

c/o Free Spirit Publishing
217 Fifth Avenue North, Suite 200
Minneapolis, MN 55401-1299
email: help4kids@freespirit.com
Web site: *www.freespirit.com*

In the meantime, have fun laughing and learning!

Ron Burgess

PART 1

Creating a Humorous Classroom

THIS SECTION WILL HELP YOU:

✓ find the humor in you and your classroom that's just waiting to be tapped

✓ create a classroom that kids will know is a fun place from the moment they walk in the door

✓ cope with classroom management, organization, discipline, and other mundane things in a humorous way

✓ get to know your students' individual talents and let them know yours.

So, as all the clichés say, don't take everything so seriously, life is too short, lighten up. Put some humor into your teaching so your kids will have laughter with their learning.

Overcoming Your Fear of Looking Foolish

Remedies for When the Joke Falls Flat

"If you let your hair down, you might be surprised what you find in it."

—BALKI BARTOKOMOUS, *PERFECT STRANGERS* SITCOM

You're thinking about taking the plunge and adding a little humor to your toolbox of teaching skills. That's great! For many people, taking that first step can be difficult. Not to mention scary. Nobody wants to look foolish, especially in front of a classroom of students. But don't let that hold you back. This chapter will give you some ideas for ways to let go of fears and take those first steps toward adding humor to your teaching.

Humor is very subjective. It isn't something that can be measured, like intelligence, and it's not something you inherit, like a big nose or goofy hair. It's something you acquire. You develop your own sense of what is or isn't funny. Your sense of humor is controlled by many things: your values, background, temperament, health, the situation at the time, the people around you, and lots of other variables. What *you* think is humorous might not be funny at all to someone else, and vice versa. Have you ever laughed so hard you cried, only to look around and see that no one else was laughing? Or sat, puzzled, while everyone around you was rolling with laughter, though you didn't get the punch line? Ouch! Well, you're not alone. And it doesn't mean your sense of humor is better or worse than the rest of the population. It's just a combination of the variables working at the time.

If you want to inject a little humor into your classroom but aren't sure where to start, take the humor quiz "What Tickles Your Funny Bone?" (page 14). Make copies to give your students, too. Invite kids to talk about their choices on the quiz. This is a great activity for loosening everyone up and it will give you some ideas of what your group finds funny.

Because so many things influence humor, some of your attempts at classroom humor are bound to bomb. So what? Hey, even the pros don't always get the laughs! Simply tell yourself that the audience's laughter zone is in a different mode than yours, and continue on. When a lesson or an idea that you've tried to teach flops, you don't go all to pieces, do you? Of course not! You review what happened, think of ways to do it differently, and try again. You can do the same with humor. Dust yourself off and get right back in the game.

Defusing the Bomb

Many people are reluctant to try using humor because they're afraid no one will laugh. It takes a healthy dose of self-esteem to put yourself in the spotlight and risk not getting a laugh. It helps to be able to laugh at yourself. As Charles Schulz, creator of the "Peanuts" comic strip once said, "The greatest gift we can give the next generation is the ability to laugh at themselves."

Attempts at being funny and not quite pulling it off, or not making it at all, can sometimes be funny in themselves. Some comedians work bombs into their routines by joking about them or using rejoinders to get a laugh. Here are some one-liners I've used that you might try when a joke falls flat:

★ "I guess you had to be there."
★ "That's the last time I'll buy a joke from the gym teacher."
★ "My three-year-old daughter thought it was funny."
★ "Did I just say that?"
★ "Later on, when you're sitting in the lunchroom, you're going to think that was so funny that milk's going to squirt out your nose."

Ask students for the one-liners they like to use, or keep track of the ones you hear them using in class.

Try It! You'll Like It!

In planning a humorous classroom, try to be receptive to new and unusual ideas that can pop up anytime and anywhere. Be on the watch for them while you're switching channels, surfing the Web, scanning a catalog, shopping for groceries, browsing in a toy store, or reading a magazine or a billboard. Let some prop, toy, thing, word, or phrase get your creative juices flowing. Change your perspective and look at things differently. If you've been operating out of a left-brain mode, switch to the right. If your creative right brain isn't coming up with anything new, switch to your regimented, steps 1-2-3 left brain. Don't be afraid to be daring!

When you come across an idea for humor, don't say, "Oh! I'd never do that." Lighten up and give it a try! What have you got to lose? Some ideas you can't or won't ever be able to use, but others you might come back to when you find a place where they'll fit. When your class is getting a little sluggish and needs a small boost, or when you feel like something is missing, try some of the suggestions in this book to add a little pizzazz. Start out small. Use one idea and see how it works. If you're comfortable with it, try others. At first, attempt only those ideas that you think are really funny. After a while, get adventurous and try something that you're not sure will work. Try one here, try one there, and before you know it, you've got the kids smiling, giggling, grinning, and laughing. Best of all, you've got them working.

Here are some ideas that have been successful in my classroom:

★ Before students arrive in the morning, write a few incorrect sentences on the board—the sillier, the better. As soon as kids arrive, set them to work making corrections. For example:

mr burgess is reelly hand some (Of course, you'd insert your name here.)

two day is the 35ed day of febuery

if you laf at this, youse as silly as me

★ In math, try inserting a joke into the equation: If you had four skunks and two more skunks came to join the party, how many skunks are stinking up your yard?

★ Silly story starters are a fun idea for a writing assignment. Give kids a strange essay title and let them add the details. Here are some of my favorites:

"Why I Like Being a German Shepherd"

"The Life Story of a School Desk"

"A Day in the Life of a Pencil"

"Things to Do While You're Waiting for the Dismissal Bell"

"Five People or Things I Would Never Want to Meet"

"25 Reasons Why I Think We Should Have School on Saturdays and Sundays"

"My Secret Identity, or No One Knows That I'm an Alien from Outer Space" (You can substitute any number of things here, like a monster, a movie star, or the principal working undercover.)

Start a Support Group: HA (Humor Anonymous)

Humor is meant to be shared. That's one of the reasons I don't like kids reading joke books during silent reading. It's too hard to stay silent! When you read a good joke you want to tell somebody. It's just more fun when you share the humor with someone else. Find other teachers and start your own humor support group. Bounce ideas around and practice new material on each other.

★ Tell each other jokes, circulate cartoons, and share funny ideas.

★ Ask what others use to get a laugh, and get their opinions on what they think is funny or how they would present a humorous idea you have.

★ Try out ideas in each others' classes. Do the presentation together for moral support. See what floats or flies or bombs.

★ Share the "Random Acts of Craziness to Add Laughter to Your Life" handout (page 15) with colleagues. Brainstorm additional crazy acts.

Become a Humor Evangelist

Spread the word about humor in the classroom and how it works to reach and motivate kids. Introduce humor to the rest of the staff. Put up funny signs, jokes, and cartoons in the teachers' lounge, on the walls in the hallway, or on your classroom door. Go for the big laugh and put funny stuff in the staff refrigerator, like a plastic banana or a rubber chicken.

Hold staff contests. Invite people to bring in their baby pictures and post them on the staff bulletin board. Try to guess who's who, and award a prize to the person who picks the most right. You could also give a prize to the baby who's prettiest, biggest, or funniest, or the one who's changed the least.

Wake Up the Kid Inside

Find out students' likes and dislikes. Watch their TV shows, listen to their music, read their books, listen to them talk to each other, and find out what riddles and jokes they laugh at.

After you gather this information, use it to your advantage. You can slant your ideas and lessons to their way of thinking. You might be able to incorporate characters from TV shows or movies in discussions. You could use or mention some of their favorite music during class. You might be able to use a popular toy or magazine for a lesson. All of this will pique kids' interest, get their attention, keep them on track, and get them smiling and learning.

Collect Your Thoughts

Start a humor journal. Get a notebook and write down your thoughts and observations on what you think is funny. Here are some journal joggers to get you started:

★ Make lists of your favorite sit-coms, movies, comic strips, cartoons, books, comedians, or funny words.

★ Write down funny lines you remember from TV shows, movies, or books.

★ Record things that amuse you and explain why you find them funny.

★ Write about people who make you laugh or smile.

★ Jot down a good joke. This will help you to remember it.

★ Record the funniest thing that ever happened to you.

★ List some of the humorous things kids say in class.

★ Paste in cartoons, comic strips, funny articles, and stories.

★ List ideas you've used that worked.

★ List ideas that bombed.

Keeping a journal will help get your ideas on humor straight in your own mind. It will also help to show how your humor is developing. A humor journal can be a great pick-me-up after (or during) a rough day. It's a good way to help you remember the positive things that have happened in your classroom. (Sometimes we tend to forget those.) Mostly it will get you thinking about and using humor.

Stop That Laughing!

Kids will laugh at almost anything. Your chalk breaks and they giggle. You mispronounce a word and they snicker. There's an unusual noise, and the whole room erupts. It's easy to feel foolish or angry, or to get embarrassed or sternly stiff when laughter happens. Try joining the fun instead. Use the laughter. Work around it. Try some funny lines like these:

★ "I think it's trying to escape" (the chalk).

★ "I meant to do that."

★ "I washed my mouth this morning and I can't do a thing with it."

★ "My tongue got stuck in my eye teeth and I couldn't see what I was saying."

★ "Is there a moose in here?"

★ "Did someone drop their false teeth?"

Humor Don'ts & a Do

Don't say you don't have a sense of humor. Everyone does. Everyone's sense of humor is unique. Just like fingerprints and snowflakes, no two are alike.

Don't be afraid of using humor. Humor, like most things in life, is not an exact science. You have to work at it and play with it to be successful.

Don't be afraid of bombing. Highly paid professionals bomb every day.

Don't let a day go by without a chance of sharing laughter with your students. Seeing kids smile and hearing them laugh shows your classroom is an inviting, fun place to be.

Do relax, grin, smile, and laugh along with your students. You've got their attention—now teach them!

What Tickles Your Funny Bone?

A Humor Quiz for Teachers & Students

1. Circle the statement you agree with:
   a. Humor doesn't belong in school.
   b. School should be more fun.
   c. There's just the right amount of humor in school.
   d. School is a joke.

2. Put a box around the answer you feel best completes the statement.
Teachers use:
   a. Enough humor.
   b. Not enough humor.
   c. Too much humor.
   d. The wrong kind of humor.
   e. What's humor?

3. Put a check mark next to the answer you agree with.
My sense of humor is:
   a. Below average.
   b. Average.
   c. Above average.
   d. I laugh at everything.
   e. I never get the joke.

4. Skip the next question.

5. When you get this far make a barking sound.

6. My all-time favorite TV comedy show or comedian is: _____

7. The funniest book I ever read is: _____

   It's about: _____

8. My favorite comic strip or cartoon is: _____

9. I think I'm funny when I: _____

10. Write everything you know about humor
in the box. Please write legibly.

Humor Box

Random Acts of Craziness to Add Laughter to Your Life

Ideas for Teachers

Try some of the following to give yourself a new outlook on life. Add some of your own. Make a checklist. Share your list with friends.

❑ Take music lessons. Not just plain old piano or guitar lessons. Try something unusual, like the accordion, tuba, bagpipes, or marimba.

❑ Take a different route to work.

❑ Listen to comedy tapes in the car or on the bus.

❑ Take flying lessons, skiing lessons, or skydiving lessons.

❑ Try skateboarding, inline skating, hot air ballooning, or flying a kite.

❑ Dust off some old skills and use them. Dig out a yo-yo, hula hoop, or jump rope and see what you can do.

❑ Try to learn how to wiggle your ears, raise one eyebrow at a time, or touch your nose with your tongue.

❑ Say hello to people you don't know. Start up a conversation.

❑ Call someone on the phone who you haven't talked to in years.

❑ Strike up a conversation when someone calls you with the wrong number.

❑ Start a book in the middle or read the ending first.

❑ Make up your own recipe, game, or song.

❑ Sing hello when you answer the phone or greet your class.

❑ Put a marking pen or crayon between your toes and try to draw.

❑ Take an adult class in clowning or stand-up comedy.

❑ Wear a red clown nose when you go out today.

❑ Play classical music for your class and lead the orchestra with your "baton" (ruler, pointer, or flyswatter). Wear a wig or a hat for added effect.

❑ Make the first thing you say to people something that will brighten their day.

❑ Face everyone when you get on an elevator.

❑ Whistle a song all the way through.

❑ Wear wild underwear.

❑ Drive your car with a puppet on your hand. Wave at people with the puppet when you stop for a red light.

❑ Think up your own acts of craziness and don't be afraid to use them.

❑ _____

❑ _____

❑ _____

If you had your life to live over, would you laugh more? Today is the first day of the REST of your life. Give laughter a chance. Start right now.

To Open Their Eyes, Organize & Be Humor Wise

Ideas for Making Your Classroom Space a Fun Place

"One person's mess is merely another person's filing system."
—Margo Kaufman

From the moment your students walk through the door, you want them to know that your classroom is a fun place. It's not just your humorous persona that will accomplish this. The classroom environment needs to *look fun*. Think about how you'd like your classroom to look and how you function best. Step back and ask yourself, "Where can I add a little color and spirit to this room?" You might even invite your students to help by suggesting ways to liven up the space.

To organize a humorous classroom, I start by putting myself and my work areas in order. I check all the organizational things that I do and look for ways to handle rules, schedules, materials, and supplies. I find it helps me to identify what's not working or needs some jazzing up. If you're like me, there are probably areas in your room that could be livened up. Don't be afraid to try something new. Apply a little creativity, ingenuity, and yes, even nuttiness to the problem, and you're sure to come up with some fun *and* funny ideas. As for those areas that are working fine, I'd suggest leaving them alone. Why mess with success?

Because you spend a great deal of time in your classroom, it should be comfortable for you. What sort of organization works best with your teaching style? Are you a super-organized Type A teacher, or do you function better with clutter? Whichever the case, it's helpful to be able to put your hands on materials when you need them.

I once had a boss whose office was the epitome of clutter. Papers were piled everywhere—on the floor, on the file cabinets, on her desk. Nowhere was there an inch of space that wasn't covered with paper. Her office looked like a total disaster. Yet, when you asked her for something, she knew exactly what pile it was in. She could retrieve anything in seconds. I suspect she was an exception to the rule, though. In my experience, most people who live with clutter tend to walk around muttering, "If I were a file folder on language arts, where would I be?"

Funny Filing

Filing isn't fun or funny, but here are some ways you can make it a little more enjoyable:

★ Most filing systems are alphabetical. Alternate ways of filing are by theme, subject, or month. For a change, try a different system. Consider using a different color for each month, theme, or subject. Use colors that are bright and uplifting: fluorescent orange for October or November (Halloween/Thanksgiving), pink for February (Valentine's Day), green for March (St. Patrick's Day), yellow for May (Spring/May Day). Use stripes or polka dots or paisley. Cover file folders with wallpaper, or leave them plain and change the dividers between subjects.

★ Add something that will give you a laugh when you open the file. Stick a funny face, a silly word, or a clever saying on the tabs. Tape a favorite cartoon to the inside cover of the file folder, or a picture of a fun activity that your class did.

★ Randomly insert in your files a few of those greeting cards that play music when you open them. You could also stuff in things that you find pleasant to touch or smell. When you open these files, you'll have a pleasant surprise and possibly a smile. And when you're feeling happy, it's easier to pass that smile along to your students.

Humorous Decor

I don't know about yours, but in my classroom even plastic plants die, so I have to use other ideas besides vegetation. Decorations won't necessarily make you laugh out loud, but they can add lightness, surprise, and grins to the room. Keeping in mind your personal taste and the learning styles of your students, you can create a pleasant and stimulating classroom environment. Here are some suggestions:

★ Bright vibrant colors can help liven up a dark corner. Fluorescent might even be better for some people. Don't be afraid to experiment. Mix colors that you normally wouldn't mix. If you want, use bright colors in smaller doses. For example, mat students' work with fluorescent paper for display or cover a couple of storage boxes with bright wrapping paper.

★ Use the Sunday comics or different types of wrapping paper as bulletin board backing.

★ Post amusing sayings or humorous pictures.

★ Decorate your file cabinet or desk. Bring in a wacky lamp you've rescued from the thrift shop. Scour garage sales for just the right set of bookends, or make your own by filling an old pair of tennis shoes with plaster and adding fancy laces.

★ Add a restaurant menu board for your lunch count.

★ Create unique room dividers from fencing, furniture, large gadgets, or gizmos.

★ Recycle unusual signs and displays, or make your own from large recycled corrugated boxes—a refrigerator box makes one of the best and biggest life-size eye catcher. Grocery stores, fast-food restaurants, and department stores have stand-up cardboard figures and signs that could be yours for the asking. They make great decorations. I had a huge, cardboard Mr. Potato Head standing at my door for years. It got loads of comments from kids and parents. I decorated him every month for the seasons or holidays. When Mr. Potato Head finally fell apart, I had to get rid of him. The first week of school, kids stopped by my room to ask what happened to Mr. Potato Head. I said solemnly, "He died." Don't ask me why but the kids thought it was hysterical, and they sent others to ask about him. I thought of other lines to give them: "He got mashed," "He ran away with a tomato," "He's out looking for a new couch."

★ Use a bathtub, rowboat, kiddie pool, inflatable boat, park bench, truck tire, decorated box, or any number of other things for a reading or lounging area. A lava lamp won't give off much light, but it will add mood to a "Rocket to Reading" area.

★ You can decorate the ceilings or floor, too. Add a plastic flamingo to a dull corner, and move it around the room occasionally. Suspend students' work from the ceiling. Put a quirky rug on the floor of your reading area, or have the kids paint a rug with grade-appropriate themes (for example, a world map, an erupting volcano, their version of a famous painting) using canvas fabric and fabric paints.

★ When decorating your room, keep in mind that visual clutter can be a problem for some children. Try to keep a balance between a classroom that's visually interesting and fun and one that's too full and chaotic. You don't have to put everything out at once. You can rotate some of your favorite decorations. That way the ideas stay fresh.

Take the Dullness Out of Cubbies, Lockers, & Desks

Sometimes classroom furniture can be, well, too functional and dull. Take lockers, desks, and cubbies, for example. What can you do to make them shout, "Hi! Welcome to a great day at school!"? Short of wiring them for sound, why don't you try some of these ideas:

★ Let the kids decorate them inside and out with photos, pictures cut from magazines, removable stickers, and their own drawings.

★ Encourage students to make signs for their cubbies, lockers, or desks. The first one most of them will hang up is "Keep Out." As they get a little more creative they might use "Enter at Your Own Risk" or "Private Property." To get kids thinking a little humorously, suggest some of these:

Three-Room Apartment for Rent

Yield

This Space for Rent; Inquire Within

Shake Well Before Using

Doctor's Office, One Flight Up

Wipe Feet Before Entering

No Parking

Deliveries in the Rear

Back Door to Superintendent's Office

Caution—Contents May Be Hazardous to Your Health

School Bus Stops Here

Don't Feed the Animals

★ If your students' cubbies, desks, and lockers currently sport their names, rename them. Kids love to have secret hiding places. Have them use their favorite hiding place names, such as:

Safe	Treasure Box	Lost in Space
Safe Deposit Box	Cave	Bird's Nest
Temple of Doom	Satellite	Space Station
Cupboard	Magic Box	Time Capsule
Secret Place	Locked Box	Buried Treasure
Black Hole	Junkyard	

Silly Signs

Humorous signs on the doors, windows, or walls are a great touch.

★ Display a sign on a window ledge full of stuffed animals: "Please don't feed the animals; they're already stuffed." "No Hunting." "Assorted Animals Crossing."

★ Attach a "Stay in School" sign to the classroom fish tank.

★ Make signs for your classroom doors, such as: "Aerobic Reading—moving our mouths, fingers, and eyes," or "Knowledge given away here—free. Bring your own container," or "Science experiment going on. Enter at your own risk."

★ Buy a reversible "Open" and "Sorry, We're Closed" sign at an office supply store to use on the door to your room. Put out a welcome mat, too.

★ Take a cue from the bakery or deli and put up a "Take a Number" sign for kids who need help or have a question.

★ Use the "Raise Your Hand" handout on page 23 and make cardboard hand shapes for each desk. If you like, have the kids make these. They may want to color and decorate the hands before cutting them out. Make stands by bending back the wrist and taping on a square of cardboard. If a child needs help, he or she puts up the hand sign and continues working. When you're finished helping one person, you can move on to the next.

★ Make cardboard signs for each desk with a happy face on one side and a sad face on the other. Encourage the kids to express their feelings.

★ Photocopy, color, and cut out the smiling lips from the "Flash a Smile" handout (page 24) and attach them to craft sticks. If someone doesn't have a smile, you can give one of yours!

Dust Off Those Collections

Collections make nice decorations, or you can use them as ice breakers or segues into lessons. Depending on the objects, you might even create specific lessons that revolve around a collection. Obvious uses for collections include counting or sorting activities, but go beyond the obvious and use your imagination. You might want to bring in your own collections (unless you collect fifteenth-century china—that's best left at home). Or, invite your students to help you start a collection for the class.

★ Cheer up a room with a collection of stuffed animals. You can have all the same such as teddies, cows, pigs, or penguins, or create a zoo-like atmosphere. Place them all over the room—on the floor, walls, tabletops, chairs, window sills, window boxes, or hanging from the ceiling in hammocks, cargo nets, or baskets.

★ Incorporate a collection of hats in your classroom. Include hats from different countries or professions. Let the kids enjoy and use them. (If your health policy doesn't allow sharing hats, try footwear instead.)

★ Hang kites, piñatas, or umbrellas from the ceiling.

★ Display pictures, photos, statues, or any other type of objects related to people or things that interest you, such as pirates, clowns, musicians, characters in history or literature, or sports figures.

★ Create a wall of pennants from cities, vacations, or sports teams.

★ Put together a bulletin board of photos, cartoons, or posters on the same theme.

★ Use boxes or containers in different colors, sizes, and shapes for your classroom storage. For example, a neat collection of new and old lunch boxes could be used to store crayons, pencils, scissors, or even snacks.

★ Show off school bells or other antique school paraphernalia bought at auctions or tag sales.

★ Display toys of one type, such as robots, dolls, trucks, boats, or doll houses. They can be useful as well as decorative. See "Toy Science" (page 111) for more ideas on incorporating toys into your lessons.

★ Include children's books from different countries and in different languages in a library collection.

★ Pull out all those apple knickknacks you've received as gifts, and incorporate the apple theme in your lessons for a day or a week:

In art, make apple prints or carve apple head dolls.

In science, identify different apple varieties. Hold a blindfolded taste test.

In math, slice up apples for a fractions unit, or calculate the number of apples in a tree or the yield of an orchard for a lesson on estimating.

In language arts, read a story or put on a play about Johnny Appleseed. Or research Sir Isaac Newton and his encounter with a falling apple or William Tell and his unique way of cutting up fruit.

In social studies, visit an apple orchard or interview an apple grower. Make apple cider.

★ Don't forget desktop collections. Decorate your desk with those little wind-up walking toys, novelty pens, pencils, pencil sharpeners, and fancy-shaped erasers.

★ Create a changeable art display using a collection of crazy refrigerator magnets. If you don't have a variety of magnets, invite students to bring in loaners for a month.

You've Only Just Begun

These are just some of the ways you can use humor to organize your classroom. Throughout this book you'll find more ideas and suggestions for humorous decorations. Once you're in "humor mode," new ideas will seem to pop up everywhere.

Raise Your Hand

A Prop for Students

Teachers: Be sure to copy this handout on heavy paper or cardstock.

Color and decorate the hand and cut it out. Fold it back along the dotted lines and tape it to a piece of cardboard to make a stand. Then, when you have a question or need help, raise the hand!

Fold under

Flash a Smile

A Prop for Teachers

Make copies on heavy paper or cardstock. Color the smiles, cut them out, and tape them to craft sticks. If someone doesn't have a smile, give them one of yours!

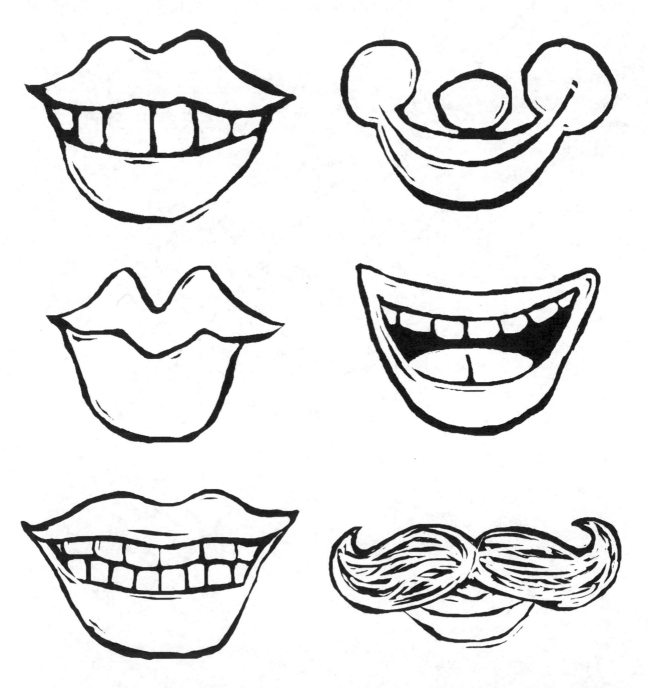

Laughter Rules!

Managing Your Classroom with Humor and Avoiding Discipline Problems

"I think the next best thing to solving a problem is finding some humor in it."
—FRANK A. CLARK

First things first. Discipline problems are no laughing matter, and they shouldn't be dealt with humorously. This book doesn't presume to offer suggestions on dishing out discipline. Discipline and discipline problems are covered by many other fine books on the market today. Some good ones to check out are listed in "Really Fun Resources," page 182 at the end of this book.

With that said, what's this chapter about? Well, it offers humorous suggestions for organizing and managing your classroom so you can *avoid* some potential discipline problems. Start the fun as soon as the kids enter the room. By incorporating humor into such mundane tasks as taking attendance and getting the lunch count, you can set a positive tone for the rest of the class time. Get the kids engaged from the outset, and chances are your day will go more smoothly. Some kids act up because they're bored. But your class doesn't need to be boring! Slip a little fun into preplanning, setting rules, going over regulations, and fine-tuning schedules, and you can help control behavior and *reduce* discipline problems. In other words, you can use humor to stop problems before they start.

Funny Rules

There may not be a lot that's funny about rules and the need for them. Still, you can lighten up and use a little humor when making and applying rules. Your main objective when establishing rules should be, "Be upbeat and smile." Try smiling while you're discussing classroom protocol with the kids. A smile will go a lot further than a stern face. If the kids perceive rules to be friendly, they might just want to observe them. While this may seem obvious, on any given day when your nerves are frayed and your mood is sinking, it's easy to get caught up in the negative and forget some of the basics.

Invite the kids to come up with some rules of their own. You'll be amazed at what they'll suggest. Some are useful, some are wise, and some are very, very funny. Kids can really get into making rules for every minute infraction, and their consequences often fall just short of beheading. (And they say teachers are tough!)

When talking over etiquette with my classes, I try to comically include all the things I don't want the kids to do. I make a list: "No hitting, punching, scratching, pinching, wrestling, pulling, pushing, poking, tripping, running, spitting, hair pulling, crying, yelling, swearing, lying, cheating, name-calling, pulling out chairs, or any other nasty thing I haven't covered." Add whatever you can think of and write it all on a long roll of paper; make sure it's long enough to reach the floor. Better yet, make it long enough to roll halfway to the back of the room! Then you can sum it all up with one rule: "In other words, respect one another."

Tattle Box

Here's an idea that has helped me curb some of the "Teacher, she cut in line" or "Teacher, he's copying" complaints. Of course, it's important to know when children are misbehaving so you can help them learn a better way to solve conflicts, but some student complaints can be trivial and use up valuable teaching time. With a tattle box, kids can put their complaints in writing and be assured that you will read them and act accordingly. Cut a slot in the cover of a shoe box (or another type of box with a lid you can lift off). Then cover the box and lid with wrapping paper to make it look nice. Label the box so students will know what it is, and place a notepad and pencil nearby.

Whenever a student feels compelled to tattle against a classmate, she or he can write the complaint on a slip of paper, sign and date it, and place it in the box. (Explain that any tattles without names and dates will be discarded.) However, before writing up a tattle, have the student apply for a tattler's license. Have on hand copies of the "Tattler's Complaint Form" from pages 33–34 for when students have a complaint. If the problem is small, by the time the student finishes filling out the application form, he or she most likely will have forgotten what the tattle was!

Check the box regularly, so you'll be aware of problems that need to be taken care of immediately. At a designated time read tattles that are appropriate for sharing at a class meeting, and invite the whole class to discuss them. Read both the serious complaints *and* the ones that seem trivial (especially several days later!), like "Tomás took my pencil," "Annie wrote on my paper," or "Michaela pushed my chair with her foot." Most likely, the class reading will reveal just how silly a lot of tattles are.

By discussing the complaints, you can encourage kids to first try to work out their disagreements with each other before coming to you for arbitration. However, let kids know that you are always available to listen to them.

Good Humor Rewards

Give kids rewards for all sorts of things: doing their homework, coming to school, helping someone, having a clean desk, turning in a neat paper, writing a complete journal page, walking quietly, picking up something, smiling, wearing a yellow shirt, remembering to raise a hand, giving the correct answer, or giving a wrong answer but still trying! A reward can be as simple as a pat on the back and a quiet word of praise or as elaborate as a special badge or certificate or a celebration. When giving out rewards, keep in mind the personality of the child. Avoid putting very shy children on the spot. Making it a big deal can quickly turn a reward into an unpleasant experience for an introverted person. Try to fit the reward to the recipient and the action. Make rewards fun for everyone.

One idea I've used is "funny money." Design your own funny money with a caricature or a picture of a current popular character (Pokémon characters, Hermione of the *Harry Potter* series, or a team mascot). Find pictures in books, magazines, book club pamphlets, or at Web sites. Photocopy the cash on green paper. (Do *not* copy real currency. The Feds frown on that.) Give the money as a reward and let students use it to buy items such as erasers, pencils, notebooks, and stickers from you. Students could exchange a certain amount of funny money for various privileges, too, such as "No Homework Tonight," "1 Cut in Line," "Lunch with a Teacher or the Principal," or "Teacher's Helper for a Day."

You can also use funny money for an auction. Collect items with book club points or from parents or tag sales. Hold an auction after a majority of the students have accumulated a sufficient amount of money. I've found that the kids will bid 30, 40, even 50 dollars in funny money for items they want. Children as young as first grade can have fun with an auction. You might even use it to help teach math concepts.

Prize Patrol

Give a prize to the person who's the quietest, to the group that forms the straightest line, or to the team who picks up the most paper off the floor. Prizes could be a lollipop, a sticker, a special privilege, or anything you want. Throw in a bouquet of fake roses and a balloon or two, and it's almost like those TV game shows!

Look who's Talking

If your students talk too much in class, you can cut down on the amount of extra chatter by using a microphone to let everyone know whose turn it is to talk. Explain that no one can talk unless she or he has the microphone, just like the audiences on the TV talk shows. You don't need a real microphone. Buy a toy one, recycle an old mike by cutting off the cord, or use a megaphone. You can also use a small plunger, a banana, or a decorated stick for a wacky microphone.

Make It into a Game

Kids enjoy games. "Simon Says" works well for many different purposes. You can use it to start or end the day or when you need to move the group from one place to another: "Simon says stand up and push in your chair. Simon says take two giant steps toward the door. Simon says WALK to the door." Or use "Simon Says" to end computer time: "Simon says log off the Internet now. Simon says let your mouse rest. Simon says put the CDs away." Play "Simon Says" to help your class clean out their desks.

For older children, make up treasure hunts or clues related to the subject they'll be studying next or to where the group is going. For example, line the class up at the door and give them the following clues to get them to their treasure or final destination.

Clue #1: Head west out of the classroom. (The class will have to decide which way is west.)

Clue #2: Go 55 steps up an ascending structure. (You'll have to determine the amount of stairs ahead of time.)

Clue #3: Keep walking until you cross a barren strip of linoleum that has an area of 500 square feet. (This could be the school lobby.)

Clue #4: Travel into a jungle of symbols and signs where information is abundant. (This could be the school library or learning center.)

Clue #5: Head east into a room where technology is at your fingertips. This is your final destination! (Destination—computer room.)

Your directions can be as specific or abstract as you want them to be. Each time you do this activity with your class, your directions can become less obvious and more challenging to figure out. You could also make a treasure hunt out of working in the library and give your group clues to find particular books or resources.

Lavatory Levity

Don't you just hate it when every other request a student makes is to use the restroom? Inevitably, during a heated discussion, someone will raise a hand and ask, "Can I go to the bathroom?"

Create a bathroom box to eliminate lavatory interruptions. Print all your students' names on small file cards; if possible, laminate them. (If you want, let the kids write and decorate their own cards.) Have students keep their name cards in their desks, or keep them in an alphabetical recipe-type box file. Remove the cover from a box with small sides (like a cigar box) and divide it into two sections by gluing in a piece of cardboard or foamcore board. Here's the fun part: you get to decorate the bottom of the inside of the box to indicate its purpose. You could make two little outhouses marked BOYS and GIRLS or two fancy bathroom doors marked LADIES and GENTLEMEN. You might want to draw bathroom stalls marked HIS and HERS.

Explain that when someone has to leave the room for the bathroom, he or she may do so without interrupting the class. All students have to do is simply put their name card in the appropriate side of the bathroom box. When they come back they take out their name card and someone else can leave. Only one boy and one girl can leave the room at a time. This way no one has to ask to leave, and you'll know where all your students are.

Goofy Attendance

There are many different things you can say to get a laugh when taking attendance. Try asking, "Whoever isn't here today, raise your hand." No matter how many times you use this line, it always gets a laugh. Other lines might include, "Who doesn't want to be here today? Raise your hand." Or, "How many people are absent today? Raise your hand."

When calling attendance, invite kids to answer with a silly word like *applesauce* or *shazzam* or *stinky feet,* instead of the usual *here.* To make it a thinking exercise have them answer using words from the same category (fruits, colors, nouns, verbs, TV shows), but without repeating what someone else has said. To make it more interesting and fair, don't call roll in alphabetical order. That way the A people won't get all the easy words and the X, Y, Z people won't always have to struggle to think of something.

The Class Is In

Another attendance-taking method is to use name cards like the ones used with the bathroom box (see page 30). Put all the name cards in a box marked OUT near the door to your classroom. Place a box labeled IN next to it. When students arrive each day they find their name cards in the OUT box and put them in the IN box. This makes taking attendance easy. Just cross-check the remaining cards with the empty seats (because some kids will always forget to put their cards in the box). At the end of the day, kids move their name cards back to the OUT box. Decorate the boxes however you'd like. OUT could be a house and IN could be a school. Or you could make a schoolroom and an outdoor scene or signs that say HERE and THERE.

Laughing Matters

Kids may giggle if they think you're having trouble, you're annoyed, or you've made a mistake. Simple things like stumbling over a word, mispronouncing a name, or sneezing can provoke gales of laughter. Your best bet is to overlook most of this chortling. Just smile or chuckle and get on with the work. By smiling and laughing yourself, you'll find it easier to get kids back on track.

The only type of humor *not* to condone is laughing *at* someone, especially in a mean-spirited way. Make it clear that laughing at people because of the way they act, look, or sound is *verboten*. Help your kids to know the difference between friendly laughter and the kind that hurts.

Keep on Smiling!

These are just some of the ways you can use humor in classroom management. You're sure to think of even more. Use what works best for you. It's hard to be funny when you're under stress, and kids pick up on that. When things seem to be getting out of hand, step back, take a deep breath, look at the situation from a different angle, count to ten (or one hundred), and smile. Chances are the kids will smile back!

Tattler's Complaint Form

Official Paperwork for Students

Please fill out the form completely and turn it in to your teacher *before* writing out a complaint for the Tattle Box.

Date: _____

Full name: _____

Street address: _____

City/State/Zip: _____

Phone number: _____

Birthdate: _____ Age: _____ Grade: _____

Favorite subject: _____

Favorite color: _____

Favorite book: _____

Parent's or guardian's name: _____

Teacher's name: _____

References (names of three people who know you):

1. _____

2. _____

3. _____

Names of people involved in the complaint:

_____

_____

_____ (MORE)

Tattler's Complaint Form (continued)

Complaint:

_____

_____

_____

_____

_____

_____

_____

_____

_____

_____

How big is the problem? Circle the appropriate number on the scale below:

TINY	KINDA SMALL	AVERAGE	SORTA BIG	REALLY MAJOR!

1	2	3	4	5	6	7	8	9	10

What action do you think should be taken? Circle the most appropriate response:

1. Apology

2. Peer mediation

3. Conference with teacher

4. Meeting with principal

5. Appearance before superintendent and Board of Education

6. Other: _____

PART 2

Pick Your Shtick

Shtick is an old Vaudeville term, taken from the Yiddish. It basically means to do your own thing, with your own props, and in a way only you can do it.

THIS SECTION WILL HELP YOU FIND WAYS
TO PICK YOUR OWN SHTICK AS YOU:

✓ explore approaches to humor using jokes and stories

✓ discover ways to use props in the classroom

✓ choose humorous ideas and routines that are right for you.

Pick one or two things that you like and try them out. See what works for you. Then slowly and surely add more. Put different things together. Try them with different subjects. Develop your own shtick.

4

Yakkity Yak!

Telling Stories & Jokes—
& Other Ways to Be Funny Out Loud

*"You can read philosophy by yourself if you want to,
but you must share a joke with someone else."*
—ROBERT LOUIS STEVENSON

Of course teaching involves talking. In fact, a good deal of your day might be devoted to verbal teaching. You use verbal skills to lead discussions, present ideas, tell stories, and give directions. The trick is to keep the kids interested in what you're talking about. A little levity can help you get your point across. This chapter offers suggestions for inserting humor into your teaching through the use of jokes, funny stories, and light-hearted conversation with the kids in your class. You've already mastered the speaking skills necessary for teaching. Now it's time to work on the funny part. You can train yourself in verbal humor, just as you were trained in other teaching skills. It's not hard. This chapter will get you started.

Kids & Jokes

Kids love jokes. Kids love corny jokes. The cornier the better. Start each day on a light note by telling a joke or two, or introduce storytime with a favorite knee-slapper. Ease pretest jitters by passing out one-liners along with the quiz sheets. Send the kids out the door with a laugh and a joke to share at home. You can read jokes from a book or tell them from memory. They don't have to fit a particular subject; they only need to get the kids laughing.

When selecting jokes, a good rule of thumb is this: the younger the kids, the cornier the jokes. Younger kids will tell a joke over and over. Older kids may moan and groan, but before the day is over they'll be telling the groaner to someone else.

Don't worry if you aren't familiar with many jokes. There are stacks of joke and riddle books in the humor section of your local library or bookstore that you can use in your classroom. Joseph Rosenbloom, a former librarian, has written dozens of books of jokes and riddles because he says these are the books children request the most. I have also written a couple of joke books that are good for elementary classes. "Really Fun Resources," pages 177–194, lists some books and other sources of jokes appropriate for use with kids. Try some of them out with your class.

Keep these things in mind if you're going to use books of jokes or riddles in your classroom:

★ Check for inappropriateness. If you plan to include joke books in your classroom library, make sure all language and subject matter is appropriate.

★ Don't try to use joke and riddle books during silent reading. No one can read a joke book silently. When you read a good joke, you just have to tell someone. Instead, you might have a joke-telling session, encourage your students to use joke books during sharing time, or suggest they take home the books and try out their favorites on their families.

★ Be mindful of the delivery. Some jokes are just a play on words. They come out better in print than they do when you tell them. For example: "Money can be lost in more ways than won" loses its impact when read aloud. If you just told the joke, few kids would catch the pun.

When telling jokes, keep in mind the age of the audience. Younger kids will laugh at almost anything. Children in first grade and younger will often try to make up their own jokes. They see and hear people laughing, but they don't quite get the idea of what a real joke is. They especially enjoy knock-knock jokes. After you tell one, they may try their own version. That's great, but be prepared for something that may not make much sense! For example, after sharing this belly-acher . . .

"Knock, knock."

"Who's there?"

"Olive!"

"Olive who?"

"Olive you!" (I love you.)

. . . you can expect to hear it told like this:

"Knock, knock."

"Who's there?"

"Olive."

"Olive who?"

"Olive on your plate!"

Hysterical laughter will follow, of course. As they get a little more knowledgeable they'll think vegetable and then change olive to lettuce or tomato. The joke becomes "Tomato. Tomato who? Tomato you," which makes no sense to anyone, including them, but they'll laugh anyway!

By second grade children start appreciating word play and jokes about familiar things. Here are some examples of jokes for this level:

"What comes after X?"

"Y."

"Why? Because I want to know."

"Why was 6 afraid?"

"Because 6 heard 7 ate 9."

Kids this age may wish to share their own jokes. They may tell you to put your finger to your head and say the letters M and T. They might get a little gross and test you with silly, tasteless jokes such as asking you to spell *pig* backwards. How you deal with this is an individual thing. Don't lose your cool. The simple reprimand, "I don't think that's appropriate," works for some people. "I don't think that's funny," or "Would your mother like to hear those jokes?" works for others. You might offer a slight chuckle and say, "Let's go on to something else," or "You can probably find funnier jokes in the humor section of the reading center." Don't get uptight; just move along to something else.

Sharing Funny Stories

You can incorporate humorous stories into the classroom in a myriad of ways. Read them aloud, act them out, or write your own stories and draw comical illustrations. You can even encourage kids to use them for book reports. Look around your classroom. You probably have a whole shelf of humor books just waiting to be used.

When sharing stories with your class, you can read them or tell them from memory. Reading the stories is a good way to start until you get over the heebie-jeebies of memorizing them. Keep these things in mind:

★ Be familiar with the story. Read it aloud to yourself before reading it to the class.

★ It's fine to use your regular voice. You don't have to use different voices or dialects unless they're your specialty.

★ Find a comfortable position, either sitting or standing. Wide gestures and movements aren't necessary.

★ Share only stories that you like personally. If you don't like the story, it will show in the telling. Start a humor file. Record in a notebook or on file cards the stories you like.

When memorizing a story, the most important thing to remember is *practice*. You don't have to memorize a story word for word. Learn only the important parts, key words, and endings. Here are some other pointers:

★ Practice makes perfect. Read the story over a couple of times. Read it out loud to yourself. Then try saying it out loud a few times without reading it.

★ Practice again using a tape recorder. Are you leaving out any essential parts? Are you speaking too quickly? Too slowly? Is your voice too soft? Too loud? Are you stumbling over or mispronouncing any words?

★ When you think you have it down pretty well, try telling the story to a family member or friend. If this person is really patient and doesn't mind hearing the same story over and over again, you can probably omit the tape recorder. (This is an especially good idea if you feel there's nothing worse than hearing your own voice.) You and another teacher could work on the same story together for your individual classes.

You can find many good books on storytelling at your local bookstore or library. One that I highly recommend is *New Handbook for Storytellers* by Caroline Feller Bauer (see page 188).

Prop Up a Story

Even a funny story can use some livening up once in a while. Sometimes the fun is in the presentation. Try using a prop or two to spice up your read-aloud time:

★ Use puppets and stuffed animals to help present stories. Some picture books come with puppets that look just like the illustrations. Use the characters in funny ways: shoulder hangers, waist huggers, shoe sitters, window watchers.

★ Paste the story on the back of a paper bag or box and slip a puppet inside through a hole in the bottom. Let the puppet "tell" the story as you read it off the back.

★ Use cards with pictures from the story on the front and key words or the whole story written on the back. (This is a great way to ease into "telling" a story rather than reading it.)

★ Consider draw-and-tell stories, cut-and-tell stories, fold-and-tell stories, or a combination of all of these. You could also try flannelboard stories, overhead stories, stories using signs and sign language, and stories using actions or sounds.

★ Cut out figures of characters from the story, attach them to sticks, and stick them into a pan of sand or on a sheet of plastic foam. As you tell the story, move the characters around in the pan or on the sheet.

★ Try a costume on for size. Dress up as the main character to tell the story. Wear a funny hat or wig or big shoes. The kids will love it! Older kids can not only learn about the story, they can also become familiar with an era's style of dress. Let kids try on part of the costume, such as a top hat or a rough collar from Elizabethan times.

"Play It Again, Sam"

Children in the younger grades love repetitive stories. The rhythm of repeated phrases or words helps move the story along. Younger children also enjoy hearing a story more than once. What child hasn't requested the same bedtime story over and over?

After hearing the story once or twice, kids love to repeat the words and noises with you. A number of popular children's authors use this repetitive device. Among them are Remy Charlip with *Fortunately,* Bernard Waber with *Ira Sleeps Over,* and Mem Fox with *Shoes from Grandpa.* Kids have a great time with the sounds in Mem Fox's *Night Noises.* My personal favorites are by Robert Munsch, who uses repetition in all of his stories, including *I Have To Go!, Show and Tell,* and *Wait and See.* (See "Fun Books for Early Elementary Children," pages 177–179, for further information.)

A book with repetition well suited for older elementary kids is *Double Trouble in Walla Walla* by Andrew Clements (see page 180). The "hodge-podge" of repetitive words will put you in a "jeepers-creepers," "wibble-wobble" word warp. After reading the story, get the kids to think of their own "root-a-toot," "mumbo-jumbo" terms. So forget the "chit-chat," "yakkity-yak" and begin.

Get the Kids into the Act

When it comes to telling stories, don't save all the fun stuff for yourself. Let the kids in your classroom get in on the humor with group storytelling. Encourage zany stories and lots of laughter.

★ Organize the class into small groups. Instruct each student in the group to choose a printed story and prepare a presentation using some of the reading and memorizing ideas from this chapter (pages 40–41). Set a time and/or length limit, and then have each student read her or his story to the group. Tell the members of the group to help each other with presentation, voice, and speed. When they're satisfied, they could do a whole class presentation or they could present their stories to another class.

★ Have group members work together to present one story, reading a paragraph each.

★ Have a group of students tell an unprepared story. Invite the students to sit in a circle. Have one person begin a story. The person can make up a beginning, read one you provide, or choose one from a familiar story. At a given signal, invite the next person in the group to pick up the story. The signal could be:

a kitchen timer or sand timer

a ball rolled from the storyteller to the person he or she chooses

a knotted string that is pulled slowly through the storyteller's hand (when the next knot is reached, the story line is passed to the right)

a preplanned word (when the storyteller uses that word in the story the next person picks up the story line)

Using Funny Lines & Silly Sayings

Bringing humor into the classroom doesn't mean doing a daily stand-up comedy routine or inserting jokes into all of your lesson plans. What it does mean is using jokes, humor, or laughter in appropriate places to help kids see that learning can be fun. Try different things. Add a line here, add a few lines there, and before you know it, you've got some funny stuff that keeps the kids alert and attentive.

Sometimes you can plan the humor. As you prepare your lesson plans, think of ways to spice them up by adding humor. You can change things around so you look at the lessons in a different way. Speech writers do the same thing. Other times the humor comes spontaneously and you just go with the flow. Many times when students start laughing, teachers try to stifle it before they find out what the laughter's about. Resist the urge to do this. Sometimes a good laugh relieves the tension or stress and gives the class a needed break.

You don't have to be a talking joke machine. Pick a couple of funny lines that you like and try to use them in a conversation with kids. As you get more comfortable, use more. Try to think of others. Write down some funny lines you've read or heard on TV or in a movie, then try to use them. A word of caution: sometimes children might be confused by humor and can react negatively to what they consider teasing. When in doubt, call attention to and laugh at yourself. Keep your conversations light-hearted, and know when to quit.

For a little help to get started in coming up with funny lines, use the reproducible form on pages 51–52, "What Can I Say When . . . ?"

You Look Good for Your Age

When you ask a student's age, act as if you didn't hear the child's answer correctly. If a child says she's six, you can reply, "You don't look sick." If a child is seven, ask, "Why are we talking about heaven?" To the child who's eight, say "Yes, I ate already." To the one who's age is nine, reply, "Why do you want to know mine? I asked yours." You get the idea.

You can also add years. When a student says eight, you can say, "You don't look 80." You could add, "You look much older" or "I hope I look that good when I'm your age."

Sometimes kids add "a half" or "three-quarters" to their ages. You could say, "I used to be seven and three-quarters. Now I'm eight and two dimes."

What's in a Name?

When you inquire what a student's name is, use a spoonerism (transpose the words.) If his name is Harold Barber call him Barrel Harbor. If she's Mary Brown, say Barry Mound. The student will correct you on the spot. Then ask, "Did you change your name? Are you sure? Double sure? Triple sure? Fourple sure?"

If someone has the same first name as a famous person, ask if they're related. For example, if a student's name is Michael, ask if he's related to Michael Jackson or Michael Jordan or Michael J. Fox.

Funny Names

Call on students using funny names or incorporate funny names into word problems. Some names that have made an appearance in my classroom include:

Klem Kaddlehopper	Hilda Hanawinkle
Karla Carlaroper	Bertha Bezzleheimer
Herby Cadingleheimer	Stella Snodgrass
Moigatroid McGilacuddy	Esmarelda Dinkledorf
Frederick Finklestein	Zelda Zoolegger

Sedwick Heffenreffer

Archibald Snazzafraz

Clarky Marlarky

Freeda Shicklegrubber

Milicent Karlafarski

Matilda Spunkenmyer

John Train's *Most Remarkable Names* (New York: Clarkson Potter Publishing, 1985) lists some very unusual real names: Katz Meow, Memory Lane, Hugh Pugh, and Orange Marmalade Lemon, to name a few. (Although this book is out-of-print, it should still be available at your public library.)

Stop Laughing!

The more you tell children to *stop* laughing, the *more* they'll laugh. You can use this to your advantage if you *want* them to laugh. Tell them that what you're doing is very serious and you want absolutely no laughing. Put on an exaggerated serious expression and look from one child to another. Scold or reprimand a few: "No laughing. I saw you giggling. Why are you giggling? This is serious stuff." This also works sometimes with sad, pouty faces. It's hard not to smile.

"Have you got the laughing bug today?" Label an empty spray bottle (the pump type, not the aerosol) with a sign that says "Laughing Bug Spray." When kids have the giggles, pretend to spray them. Tell them they really have to learn to lighten up: "You've got to be happier."

I washed My Tongue This Morning & I Can't Do a Thing with It

Show kids that you can laugh at yourself. When you've mispronounced a word or made a slip of the tongue or said something ridiculous or embarrassing, use one of the following rejoinders:

"For my next trick . . ."

"Who said that?"

"Don't try this at home. I'm a professional."

Make your tongue and mouth loose and make a noise like "blah, blah, blah," or "blub, blub, blub."

Sociable Studies

In social studies classes you can always find something to laugh at. You can tell animal jokes, mummy jokes, jokes about different countries. For instance, if you're studying the Revolutionary War, you could ask, "What did Paul Revere say at the end of his famous ride?" (Whoa!) Or "Where was the Declaration of Independence signed?" (At the bottom.) If you're studying the Civil War, you could ask, "Where did Abraham Lincoln have his mail delivered?" (His Gettysburg Address.) Of course, stay away from making fun of people or customs.

Hands Up

Use different lines for hand raising, such as, "How many are here? Raise your hand if you aren't," or "How many of you like to raise your hand? How many don't like to raise your hand? How many think raising your hand is dumb?"

Instead of raising hands, invite students to raise their right foot or left foot or little finger.

Sing It Out!

Sing out simple repetitive instructions in a different voice or with different musical styles, such as opera, Dixieland, or rap. Imagine telling the students to do simple tasks like be quiet, line up, or sit down in a strong operatic voice: "Would the class pleeeease line up at the dooooooor!"

Silly Spelling

Insert a little humor into your spelling tests. Create silly sentences to go along with the words. For instance, if the spelling word is *clever,* say, "Your teacher is very clever." If the word is *eating,* say, "I hate eating eggplant and grape jelly sandwiches."

When you're giving out spelling words, spell the word obviously wrong ("fish—Q-A-M-P") or write it incorrectly on the board. Students love to correct the teacher.

To break the monotony of the weekly spelling words, after you give the kids the required words, let them choose a few of their own. If you ask second or third graders, they'll usually choose big ones like *hippopotamus, Mississippi,* or *Massachusetts.* Throw in a really big one like *antidisestablishmentarianism* or *supercalifragilisticexpialidocious!*

Word Play

Children love word play. Tell them to use the green marker when it's obvious the marker is red. Transpose parts of words. Say posi-lutely or absi-tively. Add words together: "That tasted de-licorice." Pronounce names and subjects backwards: "Werdna, can you tell us about the seiduts laicos assignment?" (Write the backward names on the board. They'll be easier for you to pronounce and for the kids to figure out.)

I Told You a Million Times Not to Exaggerate

Kids love exaggeration. Tell them something is the biggest, best, fastest, smallest, or slowest, and you'll get a chuckle:

"this is the biggest pencil in the world."

"For lunch I had 24 hot dogs and 8 gallons of milk."

"LAST NIGHT I FLEW TO RUSSIA TO PICK THIS UP."

Silly Awards Work Both Ways

When someone has done really great work, ask for the person's autograph. In turn, let children ask for your autograph if they think you have done an exceptional job teaching, explaining, or demonstrating a lesson.

When someone gets an answer correct that everyone else has answered incorrectly, whip out the pom-poms and do a little cheerleading. "Rah, rah, sis, boom, bah!" Ham it up. Have children make mini pom-poms. Use chopsticks and thinly cut strips of streamers in a variety of colors. Tape the strips to the end of the chopstick. During certain lessons, let your class shake their pom-poms whenever someone gets an answer right.

When you announce the winner of something, do it like on the Academy Awards: "May I have the envelope, please?" (Rip open the envelope.) "And the award goes to _____." (Cue the music.) Or, let the kids put their answers in an envelope and have them announce their answers the same way. See how creative the kids become when they get to be the MC (Master of Cleverness).

Regrouped Groups

Use different names for naming groups. Don't stick to the obvious ones of A, B, C, or 1, 2, 3. Here are some alternatives: Eeny, Meeny, Miney, and Moe; Winken, Blinken, and Nod; Larry, Moe, and Curly; Aerodactyl, Ivysaur, Mew, and Pikachu. Make them all equally silly and no one will argue over which group is better.

Soup Group

When reading off the lunch list, add things to the menu. Here are some possible new entrees and side dishes: sneezeburgers, oatmeal with mushrooms, asparagus ice cream, macaroni and moldy cheese with a side order of brussels sprouts, beets, and bananas. Things like asparagus, sneezes, and beets will always get a "Yuk" or a "Gross!"—along with laughter.

I'm Sorry, That Line Is Busy

When a phone rings everyone listens. You can introduce a lesson, a book, or just a comment with a fake phone and a "person" you're talking to on the other end. You can buy a toy telephone with a real phone ring at any toy, joke, or magic store. A phone with a dangling, curly cord is funnier because kids are used to cordless and cellular phones. "Plug" the phone into some unlikely place (your desk, a book, your pocket) and start talking:

★ "Could you call back later? Everyone here is sleeping right now."

★ "No, you can't talk to Tyson, we're in the middle of class right now. . . . Are you sure it won't take too long? . . . Oh, okay! . . . Tyson it's for you. It's a girl." (If Tyson's a first or second grader, he won't come to the phone. If he's a fifth grader, it's likely that he'll not only come to the phone, but also hold a lively conversation.)

★ "Yes, this is Mr. Burgess's second grade class. Yes, there are 26 children here. No, we're not ready for gym yet."

★ "Is it really time to start the math lesson?"

★ "Hello, Mom!" (or "Dear" or "Honey" in a whiny voice). "No! I can't come home for lunch. You know I hate tofu and barley on toast. Please, can't we have something else?"

Doo-Dah, Doo-Dah

This activity is fun but it takes a little practice. Some people pick up puns and doo-dahs easily and some never get it. For information's sake, "Doo-dah" comes from the song "Camptown Races": "Camptown ladies sing this song. Doo-dah, doo-dah." When you or someone else says something that has seven or eight syllables, you add "doo-dah, doo-dah." Most of the time you can pick it up easily. It's kind of a rhythm thing that you hear.

"Take your pen and write this down. Doo-dah, doo-dah."

"Everyone stand and face the front. Doo-dah, doo-dah."

"May I go to the bathroom now? Doo-dah, doo-dah."

"Oh, wow, this is so much fun! Doo-dah, doo-dah."

"Now you have to work on it. Doo-dah, doo-dah."

Ask your class if they can think of other songs that would work like this.

A Final word

When you think of something funny, say it. Don't worry if it doesn't get a laugh. Continue on with what you were doing. If a student says something funny and the class laughs, laugh along with them, and then continue on with what you were doing.

There are many humorous words and lines you can use to make your classroom fun. You don't have to do a stand-up comedy routine. Simply look for things that will get a chuckle or a grin or even a groan. Use them to lighten up the moment and give learning a lift!

what Can I Say when...?

A Worksheet for Teachers

Do students keep asking the same questions over and over again? Are there little annoyances you wish to nip in the bud? Here are some humorous responses that will get results and a smile, too. (There's even space to add some funny lines of your own!)

what can I say when...

... someone asks, "Do we *have* to do this?"

"Yes, we have to do this because it says we do right here in the teacher's manual."

"If we don't, the principal will come down and we'll all have to copy the dictionary."

_____

_____

_____

_____

... the kid in the third row keeps tapping her pencil on her desk?

"Is that Morse code?"

"Listen! Someone's sending us a message."

"Are you practicing for your tap dancing lessons?"

_____

_____

_____

_____

... a paper airplane nearly clips my ear?

"Have you joined the Air Force?"

"I think we're being invaded by alien flying saucers."

"Wow, the mosquitoes are big in here."

_____

_____

_____

_____

(MORE)

what Can I Say when...? (continued)

Write some requests you hear often. Think of some funny answers that will get a giggle or a laugh.

"_____?"

_____

_____

_____

_____

_____

"_____?"

_____

_____

_____

_____

_____

"_____?"

_____

_____

_____

_____

_____

"_____?"

_____

_____

_____

_____

_____

Humor Helpers

Using Props, Costumes, Special Events, & Other Funny Stuff

"Good teaching is one-fourth preparation
and three-fourths theater."
—GAIL GODWIN

Sometimes it's just easier to be funny if you have a prop of some kind. Items like chattering teeth, goofy glasses and hats, and the arrow-through-your-head gimmick can add laughter to your lessons without your saying a word. You can use props to introduce themes, recognize special events, or simply break up the classroom routine.

Consider trying the following humorous suggestions for props, costumes, and special occasions. You can adapt them for nearly any subject or classroom. They are simple changes or additions that'll help you find funny and effective ways of reaching kids. With a little concentration, ingenuity, and persistence, you're sure to find uses for props in your teaching.

Put Together a Prop Box

Decorate a large cardboard storage box to fill with all your different costumes, hats, and other assorted classroom props. You might label it, "Teacher's Treasure Box of Laughs" or "Use Only in Emergencies." Position the box in a convenient place in your room, and dig into it whenever you need a prop for a laugh. Here are some suggestions to get you started:

★ Include some larger-than-life items, such as giant scissors, inflatable crayons, and oversized pencils, erasers, flyswatters, and eyeglasses. Big pencils and crayons make excellent pointers. A big eraser can take care of all those big mistakes. Put on a pair of oversized specs when it's time to read aloud and you're sure to get a laugh. Bothered by a pesky fly? Haul out that huge fly swatter.

★ Try mini props for a quick chuckle. Use a tiny hand as a "microwave," or read a "short story" from a miniature book.

★ Throw in some large rubber ears glued or taped to an earmuff. You can put them on to signal when you can't hear over all the commotion.

★ Include a big foam "We're #1!" hand like those you see at sporting events. When you need the class to be quiet, hold it up to your lips.

★ Put in a set of bumblebee antennae for when you want kids to "listen up."

★ Don't forget a pair of glasses with a fake nose attached and a red clown nose. Use them just to get the kids' attention.

★ Include an inflatable alien doll to use when you present a new and strange concept or an activity that's really out of this world.

★ Add a zippered banana for lunchtime humor. You can unzip it, take out a pickle, and declare, "I love these green bananas!"

★ Leave some space for assorted footwear, headgear, and other costume pieces you think would perk up your class time.

★ Check out some of the off-beat items you can pick up at toy stores and novelty shops. See "Really Fun Resources," pages 188–194, for a listing of catalog companies and Web sites where you can find novelty items.

It's in the Bag

Recycle those fancy gift bags that are too pretty to throw away. Use them to introduce a book or a subject. Paste a picture about your project on the front, attach your outline or "cheat sheet" to the back, put inside any props or items you might need for the lesson, and you're all set. You can introduce any subject with simple little props pulled out of a bag. For example:

★ a robot or insects for science

★ a costumed doll or a map for social studies

★ a clock, a calculator, or money for math

★ a small skeleton or stethoscope for health

★ flower seeds for Barbara Cooney's *Miss Rumphius,* a cookie for Laura Joffe Numeroff's *If You Give a Mouse a Cookie,* or a magic wand for J.K. Rowling's *Harry Potter* books in reading (see pages 177, 178, and 181)

★ a CD or mouse for computer class (add big wiggle eyes to the mouse for added fun!)

★ a set of magnetic letters for spelling

Mystery Boxes

Let a box (wrapped or unwrapped) sit mysteriously on your desk. When you wish to introduce a lesson theme, open the box with great fanfare to reveal a secret prop inside. Then use the prop to introduce the subject.

Or, use a series of boxes to heighten the mystery. Place a small item pertaining to the subject inside the smallest box. Wrap the box and place it inside a slightly bigger box and wrap that one. Do this two or three more times. Then, as you introduce the subject, begin unwrapping the boxes. The suspense will build with each new box. If you want, use the wrapping paper on each box to give clues about your topic.

You could do this same activity using bags. Use different sizes, shapes, or textures of bags and different kinds of stuffing, such as tissue, newspaper, or cloth.

A Library of Laughs

You can use books as props in a couple of ways. For example, cover an oversized book with a fancy book cover or create a large "book" by taping together two pieces of cardboard. Write your topic on the front cover in a humorous way, such as "Half of Everything You Always Wanted to Know About Fractions" or "Spelling from Aardvark to Zymurgy." Then put down the information you want to talk about on a card and clip it to a page inside the book so that it's easy to open to the right place. If you go the cardboard route, simply write or tape the information inside.

Or, create a book with a secret hiding place like the ones you've read about in mystery stories. Buy an old hardcover book at a yard sale or thrift store. They don't cost much. Choose a really thick one. Leave a few pages in front and a few pages in back and hollow out the rest of the book. Leaving a one-inch border all around, cut through the pages with a razor knife. You can do quite a few pages at a time. Once you've hollowed out the book, make an appropriate book cover and put items that pertain to your subject in the secret hiding place. This prop works really well to introduce stories. If you're reading Maurice Sendak's *Chicken Soup with Rice,* you could put a packet of soup in the book. For Byrd Baylor's *Everybody Needs a Rock,* stick in—you guessed it—a rock.

For an older audience, try something a little more symbolic. For example, for E.B. White's *Charlotte's Web,* stick in things to represent the written items that Templeton the rat finds for Charlotte's web, like an ad with the word *crunchy* or a clothing tag that says *preshrunk* on it. Or, stick in something that helps to resolve the story, like a dog whistle for David A. Adler's *Cam Jansen and the Mystery of the Dinosaur Bones* (see "Really Fun Resources," pages 177–181, for more information and book ideas).

If the book is thick enough, you might put a small tape recorder in the hollow. It could play scary music or a witch's laugh to go along with monster or ghost stories, or sound effects and background music to accompany your reading of any story.

Packed & Ready to Go

Suitcases or old steamer trunks make great props. The bigger, the better. Haul a large suitcase into class (or walk to a closet and take one out), go to your desk, plop the suitcase on top and open it to reveal . . . one little item about the subject you're teaching or a book that you want to present. Take out the item, close up the suitcase, drop it on the floor, and continue on as if nothing has happened. It's sure to get the kids' interest.

Attention, Please!

You can use props to gain attention or to get a slightly boisterous class back on track. Some teachers use a musical chord or a series of notes on the piano to gain the class's attention. Others clap a rhythm. Some flick the lights or ring a bell. Add a little creativity and try a wooden train whistle or a duck call. Or how about a bird warbler—the plastic ones that you put water in and blow. A toy trumpet, a kazoo, or any other toy instrument would be good. Holding up a stop sign or a picture of a stoplight could also work.

Humorous Head Attire

As with the old sayings "Put on your thinking caps" or "Changing hats," you can put on a hat for different subjects. A hat can help you highlight a theme or simply change modes. You can use one hat with interchangeable signs for a number of topics. Print titles on several 3" x 5" file cards. Attach one side of a fabric fastener strip (such as Velcro) to the front of a baseball cap. Put the other side of the fastener strip on the back of the cards. Then you can easily attach them to the cap and change them in an instant. Here are some sign suggestions for your cap:

★ Thinking Cap (You could make one for everybody.)

★ Reading Coach

★ Science Professor

★ Desk Inspector

★ Room Inspector

★ SHHH (to signal silence) and Talking Allowed (to let kids know when they can talk)

In addition to the changeable hat, try these on for size:

★ a silly umbrella hat for a science unit on weather

★ a hat that you and the kids have designed

★ a dunce cap for when YOU, not the student, make a mistake

★ a wizard's hat to use when someone has done or said something exceptional

"The Winner for Best Costume Goes to..."

You can use costumes or hats from the prop box for different subjects or themes. Try some of these:

★ Wear a lab coat for a science presentation. You could also wear one and carry a paint pallet when presenting an art lesson.

★ Put on a crown and robe and dress like a pharaoh for a unit on Egypt. Or, wrap yourself like a mummy. Encourage your students to try on costumes, too.

★ Don a chef's hat for a cooking class or when reading books that mention cooking. You could also make unusual sandwiches, real or imaginary.

★ Use cheerleading pom-poms to lead a cheer for a book, book character, or subject.

★ Dress like a book character or wear a hat or a mask of the character as you read a book or a series of books. You might put on a sunbonnet and wire-rimmed glasses when reading Mother Goose rhymes, wear a ten-gallon hat for western stories, or stick on a pair of mouse ears when reading aloud Beverly Cleary's *Ralph S. Mouse* or E.B. White's *Stuart Little.*

★ Dress as an author or a famous person. Older students might enjoy researching a person's life, writing a short biography, and then dressing like the person as they give a presentation. You might even do presentations for other classes. Begin with easy characters, such as Ben Franklin, Betsy Ross, George Washington, Abraham Lincoln, Mark Twain, and work up to people like Albert Einstein, Amelia Earhart, Thomas Edison, Eleanor Roosevelt, Edgar Allen Poe, Marie Curie, and Galileo. Researching, dressing like, and presenting Dr. Seuss would also be a great project.

★ Dress as royalty and teach the whole class as a queen or king for a day. You might try dressing as The King—Elvis. How would Elvis teach?

★ Brainstorm how a witch, a pilgrim, a pirate, or a movie or book character would teach for a day. Then dress as one of them.

★ Have kids research a famous person and decide how that person would teach. For example, would relaxed-mannered Thomas Jefferson wear his slippers to school? Since he initiated the handshake rather than bowing to the president, would he drop the formality of calling a teacher Mr. or Ms.? Would Oprah or Rosie O'Donnell just talk, talk, talk?

The costume and presentation ideas are endless: a police officer when studying laws, a firefighter for fire safety, a conductor for music, a knight from King Arthur's Round Table, a witch from the witch trials. Every subject, topic, theme, or book will suggest its own particular costume.

Accessorize!

You aren't the costume type? Well, you can still add some humor with what you wear. Call it Classroom Casual. The selection ranges from humorous watches, jewelry, and pins to ties, sweaters, and sweatshirts. Kids really appreciate when adults wear funny things like cartoon character watches or sweatshirts with silly sayings on them. You can find jewelry, sweaters, and sweatshirts for all the different holidays and seasons, not to mention some great cartoon, movie, and TV character ties. You don't have to dress like a clown to get a smile.

Come to the Party!

Most elementary classes have parties for holidays and birthdays. Don't limit your parties to those events only. Try celebrating some different occasions:

★ Have a party for a book character. What day would be her or his birthday? What would you have for decorations, food, and games? Who would you invite?

★ Plan a party for the president, a well-known scientist or author, or some other famous or near-famous personality. Let the kids choose the person and do some research. If the individual you're celebrating is living, you might send an invitation to the party or a letter explaining what you have planned. But be sure to let students know that the guest is unlikely to attend.

What's Today?

Set aside a day once in a while as a "Special Theme Day." Everything done on that day—stories, songs, games, books, artwork, science projects, and lessons—relates to the day's chosen theme.

You could hold Slippers Day, Western Day, Sunglasses Day, Favorite Color Day, Stuffed Animal Day, Beach Day (in the winter), Snow Day (in the summer), Silly Socks Day, Joke Day, or Inside-Out Day. Here are some more suggestions, along with some ideas for projects:

★ **Hat Day.** Everyone wears different types of hats. Make hats. Have a hat fashion show. Research the history of hats. Discuss the many uses and kinds of hats.

★ **Clown Day.** Dress like clowns or do clown makeup. Read stories that have clowns in them. Arrange for a clown visitor.

★ **Royalty Day.** Everyone dresses as a king, queen, prince, or princess. Stories, books, and activities during the day center around knights, castles, kings, and queens.

★ **Awards Day.** Give out silly awards all day long. Give awards to the person who has the longest name or brightest smile, is the first to the door every day, uses the pencil sharpener the most, falls out of her chair the most, answers the most questions, raises his hand the most, drops her pencil the most—the list could go on and on. Make up some funny award certificates or design humorous trophies. Send everyone home with an award.

★ **April Fools' Day.** Don't celebrate in April, though. That's much too predictable. Celebrate in March or September or some other month. You might research the history of April Fools' Day. Where and when did it start? How did it get its name?

★ **Mismatched Shoes Day.** Encourage everyone to wear shoes that don't match. (Socks work well for this, too.) Study footwear. Read *The Foot Book* by Dr. Seuss (see page 179). Make sock puppets.

★ **T-shirt Day.** Invite everyone to wear a T-shirt with pictures on it. The pictures could be of a specific thing such as animals, boats, or cars. Work the pictures into your lessons for the day.

★ **Autograph a T-shirt Day.** Ask everyone to bring a plain T-shirt to class. Then let students autograph each others' shirts or decorate their own. Write poems or riddles on the shirts during language arts, or equations during math. During art time, you could paint, stencil, or tie-dye the shirts.

★ **Popcorn Day.** Make popcorn and eat it. Play games like "Popcorn Toss" (yes, it's messy!) or "Popcorn Bingo." Make collages or pictures with popcorn. Create popcorn decorations. Read popcorn stories and books.

★ **Balloon Day.** Have on hand all different types of balloons—long, short, big, small, helium, air. Play "Balloon Toss" and hold balloon relays. Do science projects on balloons and air pressure. Study the accomplishments of some hot-air balloonists. Decorate balloons. Make balloon people or animals. Write questions or activities on balloons. Invite a balloon vendor to come to the school.

★ **Forward/Backward Day.** Half the class spends the day doing things forward. The other half of the class does things backward. For instance, the forward group would complete an assignment from the beginning, the backward group would start at the end and work their way to the beginning. You might allow the kids to wear their clothes backward. To make things really challenging, have the backward group walk backward. Half-way through the day, the class reverses roles.

That's the Ticket!

Everyone knows that if you need a ticket to get in to see something, it must be important or special. Buy a roll of tickets at a stationery or party goods store. Use the tickets to introduce a special classroom event or special topic. Pass out tickets to all the kids and have them stand outside the door. Then put on your ticket-taker cap and start collecting. Rip the tickets in half or stamp them.

TV Time

Do a whole lesson or theme or test as a television show. Phrase test questions (or answers) like those on *Jeopardy!* or on quiz shows that are geared especially for kids, such as *Figure It Out* on Nickelodeon.

You might invite older kids to create a newscast or documentary centered around a book character or famous people in history, places in world geography, or science facts. Include some commercials to break up the program. You could even videotape the whole thing to show at a parent open house or PTA meeting. Use the sample script, "WACKY News Script" (pages 66–67), to get your class started. Invite volunteers to read the script through once, in character. Then go through the script again, talking about ways they could write their own scripts. When you think they're ready, have them work in small groups to create scripts for an area of study.

Do You Believe in Magic?

Magic can be fascinating. Even though most school-age kids realize it's all a trick, the fascination doesn't go away. Many kids will try to figure out how it's done. You can capitalize on this interest by using magic in the classroom. Find tricks you can use with a story or book you're teaching. Introduce math ideas, especially money and time, using coin and card tricks. You'll also find that many magic tricks are based on scientific principles. I use magic tricks during show and tell or sharing time. They really get the kids talking. Once you get started, the ideas are limitless.

You can find books of magic tricks at the public library, your school library, or your local bookstore. A good starter magic book is *The Magic Handbook* by Peter Eldin. This book and others are listed in "Magic," pages 184–185. Some teacher catalogs have books on using magic to teach science and math. Magic companies, listed in the catalog section (see pages 188–191), are another source of catalogs that offer great reading and many ideas. The catalogs cost from six to twelve dollars, a bargain when you consider that they're usually the size of a telephone directory.

Some of the magic tricks I've used are a dove pan or a change bag for producing things used with books or lessons, a small change purse for producing money, and decks of trick cards to work with adding, subtracting, and multiplying. I've used magic to teach lessons on gravity, air pressure, optical illusions, magnets, food, sound, motion, bugs, animals, and ecology, to name a few.

When performing a magic trick, what really sells the trick and makes it useful is the "patter." Patter is entertainer's talk for the story that sets up the trick. Your patter will differ depending on your subject and the age of your students. You can use the same trick for different subjects just by changing the patter or setup. With a little practice, ingenuity, and patter you can add fun and excitement to a lesson. You'll hold the kids' attention like magic!

Abracadabra!

Every great magician and teacher needs a magic wand. You can wave it over a science experiment, use it to conjure up a math answer, or make it into a really cool pointer.

You can buy a wand at a magic shop, or you can make one from a black plastic golf-club holder and a couple of aspirin bottles. The golf-club holder will cost around two dollars and will be about three feet long. Cut it down to around 18 to 20 inches with a craft knife or sharp scissors.

← Cut to 18–20 inches →

For the wand's white ends, cut off the bottom of two white plastic aspirin bottles. The bottle bottoms usually will fit snugly over the golf-club holder. If they're slightly big, wrap some black electrical tape around the ends of the golf-club holder. Don't tape the bottle ends on; you want to be able to take them off. If the bottles are a snug fit on the wand, you can push one end on hard and the other end will pop off. It's a pretty funny effect and gets a lot of laughs.

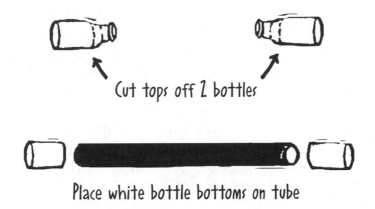

Cut tops off 2 bottles

Place white bottle bottoms on tube

When you've finished creating the wand, you can roll up lesson plans or a visual aid for a lesson and stick it inside the wand. When it's time for the lesson, you can wave the magic wand and pull out the information. Or, fill the wand with confetti, and before the lesson ask, "Can you feel the magic? There's magic in this room!" Secretly remove the cap on the wand and wave it around. Confetti "magic" will fly everywhere! (The whole class can help with cleanup.)

 Juggling

With a beginner's book from the library or a magic supply store you can learn basic juggling. You don't have to work up a professional act or buy expensive material. Most juggling books start with scarf juggling. It's easy because the scarves are lightweight and they fall more slowly than other objects. It takes some practice, but once you learn how, you can teach the kids.

You can buy many other juggling props at a toy store. Once you master scarves, move on to tennis balls, bean bags, or even sets of devil sticks.

Don't forget the patter as you juggle. Talk about how hard it is to juggle things in your head, like the components of a story, the characters and dates in a history lesson, different math symbols, or even the food chain.

It's a Balancing Act

Balancing is part of juggling and is also very easy to learn with a little practice. With balancing, the thing to remember is, the taller the object, the easier it is to balance. A pencil or a straw is almost impossible to balance on your finger, but a yardstick is easy. A broom is even easier. Keep your eye on the top and move your hand to compensate for the falling. If you're balancing something on your chin, move your body to compensate.

For an especially easy balancing trick, place a dab of rubber cement on the end of your nose and a dab on the bottom of a paper cup. Let it dry. It won't be noticeable to the kids. Tell your class that you're going to attempt to balance the paper cup on your nose. Lean your head back and place the cup on your nose. (Move your head back and forth to imitate balancing.) *Ta-dah!* After a minute or two, tip your head up and look at the class. The cup will stick straight out in front you, still attached to your nose. The kids will love it.

Peacock feathers—or any other long feathers—are great to practice with. If you have enough, the whole class can balance at the same time.

Your patter during a balancing act could be about balancing schoolwork, gravity, or motion; keeping everything in your story balanced; keeping your eye on what's important; or a hundred other things.

Catalog Shopping

Catalogs and junk mail have many uses in the classroom. You can use them in math for simulated buying sprees with a specified amount of money. You can use them for art references or collages. But most of all, you can use them for just plain fun.

Catalogs and magazines exist for every conceivable topic under the sun. There are even catalogs of catalogs. Check out the list of catalogs, pages 188–191, for more information, or read magazines and books on subjects that interest you to find additional catalogs or organizations. They usually will have a section on organizations and suppliers. The classified sections in the back of *Popular Science* and *Popular Mechanics* advertise many different suppliers and organizations. You can also check out a subject on the Internet. You'll find more information than you'll know what to do with.

A Word of Encouragement

There are many different ways to bring humor into your classroom. Props, costumes, magic, and juggling might seem a little over the top for some teachers. All teachers aren't extroverts, and some of the ideas in this book will work better for some folks than others. But I hope the ideas inspire you to try new things with your students. Be daring. Look around. Experiment. What do other people do? What do the kids like? Be innovative. What makes *you* giggle, chuckle, chortle, or snort? Use it!

WACKY News Script

A Sample Script for Teachers & Students

ANCHOR: Good morning. Welcome to the W-A-C-K-Y Early Edition of the news. I'm _____. In overnight news, we have reports of a wolf harassing a neighborhood. We switch you now to a live update from _____, our reporter on the scene. _____?

REPORTER: Good morning, _____. As you can see from the wreckage of a straw house behind me, this neighborhood was ransacked overnight. Authorities have confirmed that they are looking for a suspect fitting the description of a large gray wolf with beady eyes. Witnesses say the wolf literally blew down the house you see here. Fortunately, no one appears to have been home at the time. It is not known why the wolf destroyed the home. According to local police, several other homes in the area have been damaged. We'll try to get footage of this for our later broadcast. This is _____ reporting from Pig Town. Back to you, _____.

ANCHOR: Thank you, _____. In other news, officials at NASA have released photographs taken by the Hubble space telescope of what looks strangely like a cow jumping over the moon. Scientists give no explanation for the photos, noting that further study is necessary.

When we return, _____ will join us with today's forecast. Please stay tuned.

COMMERCIAL ANNOUNCER: This morning's class is brought to you by ForestGroup.com, where trees are much more than just a natural resource.

(MORE)

WACKY News Script (continued)

ADVERTISEMENT: Hi! I'm Samantha Squirrel and I'd like to talk to you about my friend here, Mr. Woody Willow. Woody's a little unhappy these days because he doesn't feel he's getting the respect he deserves. It's enough to make a grown tree cry. You see, trees like Woody are very giving plants. They're a vital resource for all living things, providing shelter and building materials and even really good food. (I especially like the nuts I get around the holidays!) Ask any tree and it'll give you the wood right off its back. So how can we help lift Woody's spirits? Well, pay attention to the trees around you. Water them, pamper them, even hug a tree once in a while. Remember, trees are our friends.

ANCHOR: Welcome back to W-A-C-K-Y's Early Edition. It looks like we're going to see some changes in the weather. Meteorologist _____ is here to fill us in on all the details.

WEATHER PERSON: That's right, _____. As you can see from the weather map, today is starting out mostly sunny but partly cloudy. I hope you brought your umbrella with you because by early afternoon it's going to be raining cats and dogs. Watch out that you don't step in a poodle on the way home today.

ANCHOR: Thanks for the advice, _____. Now on to more of this morning's top stories . . .

6
On with the Show!

Perk Up Your Teaching with Puppets

"Try not to have a good time. . . .
This is supposed to be educational."
—CHARLES SCHULZ

Puppets are wonderful props to use in the classroom. They're entertaining and they make great teaching tools. You can use puppets to enhance all curriculum areas, not just drama and art. They're a surefire way to bring humor into any situation, because children easily identify with them, and they make learning fun.

This chapter contains many suggestions and ideas for creatively incorporating puppets into your teaching. You don't need to limit the use of puppets to classes of young children, either. While young children especially identify with puppets, you can use puppets effectively with all ages, both in regular and special education class settings. Older kids will enjoy creating their own puppets, especially those that are more complicated or larger-than-life. Marionettes and life-size papier mâché puppets are good candidates for use with older kids. Hand puppets are perennial favorites among the younger classes.

You can buy your own puppets or make them. Store-bought puppets can be fun, and in some cases are more effective than the homemade variety. Children relate to their realistic appearance, especially the animal puppets. But puppets from the store can be quite expensive, so if you're watching your pocketbook, you may want to check into making your own. This chapter will show you how.

Nontraditional Puppets

Don't know how to sew? Don't have the right materials? Don't have time? Don't have enough money to buy that elaborate puppet you saw at the mall? Don't worry! You can turn lots of stuff into puppets. Check out these "not-the-norm" ideas:

★ Use stuffed animals. Hold them up and move and jiggle them as the puppet speaks. What could be more simple?

★ Stick your hands into two shoes and start them talking. One could be male and the other female.

★ Attach a paper smile to a pair of blunt scissors or draw faces on a coffee cup and a spoon.

★ Make large puppets from a mop and a broom.

★ Use a hat, ball, box, or almost anything on a stick.

★ Draw a face on the side of your fist and let your hand do the talking for you.

★ Use a large paper yard-waste bag to make a larger-than-life puppet. Put the bag over your head and mark where eye, mouth, and arm holes should be. Take off the bag and cut out the holes. Draw a face that takes up about two-thirds of the bag and add yarn or string for hair. The puppet could be a caricature of a famous person.

yarn or paper strips for hair

eye and mouth holes

big face
(⅓ of bag)

large paper
yard-waste bag
(about 3 feet long)

little body

Making Puppets

Try puppet construction for an enjoyable project to add humor to the day. It's a fun activity that you can do on many levels, from very simple to very elaborate and with younger kids or older ones. The following ideas only scratch the surface of puppet construction. Numerous books on puppet making are available at your local library or bookstore. (See "Puppets," page 187, to read about a few.)

The Smorgasbord Method

Accumulate a box of disposable items: paper towel rolls, paper plates and cups, boxes of all kinds, chenille stems (pipe cleaners), egg cartons, plastic utensils, gloves, socks, mittens, Ping-Pong balls, Styrofoam shapes, Styrofoam packaging, sponges, pins, paper clips, elastic bands, dowels, beads, bangles, sequins, plastic hosiery eggs, and craft sticks. Include scraps of yarn, string, fabric, felt, rugs, wallpaper, tissue paper, foil, and gift wrap. This box of treasures should help to stimulate imagination.

After gathering the raw materials, your class can proceed to assemble puppets using one of the following approaches:

★ Set out all the materials with simple instructions to create a puppet. (See "Make Your Own Hand Puppet," page 78.)

★ Create puppets for a story students have written or read.

★ Display a sample puppet made with the shown materials and then let the kids make their own.

★ Show many puppets made from the materials and encourage students to come up with more ideas.

★ Pick one type of material and demonstrate how to use it to make a puppet.

I've used all of these approaches and they all work. Creative participation will depend on the age of the participants and enthusiasm (yours and theirs). However, placing everything out at the beginning might overwhelm some students. Working through one or two types of material at a time seems to be the best approach. Once the children get the hang of using different types of material, they become more creative, and their puppets will be as different from one another as the children who create them.

Quickie Puppets

The following are a few ideas—okay, quite a few—for making quick puppets.

★ Create a puppet with a paper lunch bag.

★ Assemble puppets from paper plates and cups or plastic and wooden utensils.

★ Create a dragon or an alligator from an egg carton.

★ Construct talking mouth puppets from boxes and tubes (cereal, laundry detergent, toothpaste, pudding boxes, or paper towel or bathroom tissue rolls). You can also make a talking mouth puppet by placing your hand in the bottom of an envelope. Put your thumb in one corner and fingers in the other corner.

tissue box

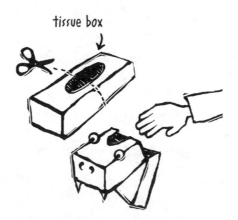

★ Make a puppet head from a paperbag stuffed with newspaper and attach it to a stick.

★ Glue a Styrofoam ball head to a detergent bottle on a stick.

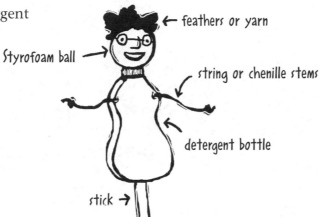

feathers or yarn →

Styrofoam ball →

string or chenille stems

detergent bottle

stick →

★ Paint finger puppets on your fingers.

★ Use a sock (preferably a clean one) or a slipper.

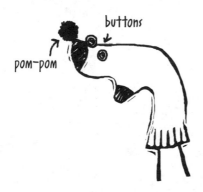

buttons

pom-pom →

★ Create a quickie puppet with changeable Styrofoam or rubber ball heads. (Use the pattern on "Make Your Own Hand Puppet," pages 78–79, to make the body.)

★ Decorate a Styrofoam ball or a potato with eyes, a nose, a mouth, and hair. You could use Mr. Potato Head parts or make your own.

★ Use hook and loop fastener strips (such as Velcro) on cloth puppets so you can change hair, eyes, mouths, and ears simply by tearing off one and applying a new part.

★ Decorate mops, brooms, or feather dusters with wiggle eyes, Ping-Pong ball eyes, sunglasses, or Groucho eyeglasses and nose.

★ Cut two-inch squares from paper or felt and attach them to pencil tops. Glue on or draw facial features.

★ Draw a face on an aspirin bottle or a juice bottle with permanent marker and stick it on your finger.

All the World's a Stage

Stages for your puppet performances can be as simple or as elaborate as you want. You can use:

★ the top of a table or desk

★ an overturned chair or table

★ a cloth tacked up between two chairs or a doorway

★ boxes, bags, hats, or baskets with holes in the bottom for your hand to go through as you hold it in your lap

★ a soap box with a hole in the bottom for a "soap opera"

★ a large empty picture frame hung from the ceiling with string at the correct height (leave the rest up to the imagination)

Or you can build a very complex stage in the shape of a castle, fort, spaceship, house, truck, or boat.

Puppet Pointers

Here are a few simple things to remember when you or your students are using puppets:

★ **Voice.** Each puppet should have its own distinct voice that is slightly different from your own. Don't make it a high squeaky voice that no one can understand, or a voice that's hard on your throat. If you're using a puppet stage, speak loudly because your voice will be muffled behind the set.

★ **Eye contact.** If you're using a puppet without a stage, look at the puppet when it's talking. Try not to have your puppet's eyes looking at the ceiling or floor.

★ **Movement.** When moving a puppet around on stage, have it walk as if it has feet, and avoid zipping it around like it is a high-speed robot. When a puppet is talking, move its mouth and body in an exaggerated way. If there are two puppets on a stage, move the talking puppet while the other puppet stands still and watches the one talking.

★ **Position.** Keep in mind the puppet's position. Try to maintain the same puppet height throughout the performance. Don't allow your puppet to sink into the stage, and avoid letting it lean at an odd angle or hang onto the stage with its chin.

★ **Scripts.** Many of your shows or puppet "happenings" will be improvisational or ad lib, but if you're using a script, it works best to prerecord the show or let someone narrate it. Trying to read a script and remembering puppet placement and movement at the same time is very difficult.

Teaching with Puppets

Puppets can add humor to the teaching of any academic subject. Plus, they can help you develop kids' social skills, arbitrate disagreements, and increase your effectiveness as a teacher. How? Consider these ideas:

★ Boost your classroom management with puppets. Young children may respond more easily and positively to commands from a puppet.

★ Add zest to a science unit by including a puppet "expert." Use an animal, a bird, or an insect to teach about trees, weeds, plant life, ecology, survival, biology, or any number of things. For example, a whale puppet could teach about whale migration, whale extinction, whale stories, whale songs, whale facts, and whale statistics.

★ Let a farmer puppet teach about seeds, plants, growing, farming, vitamins, tools, the "olden days," or folklore.

★ Invite a group of alien puppets to teach about space, rockets, planets, time, science, and science fiction. The puppets could even help teach writing and spelling by asking questions about English spelling and usage.

★ Use puppets from different countries to teach about travel, geography, foreign language, cultural stories, and fables. The puppets could answer many questions about the cultures they represent.

★ Employ the use of puppets to help children understand learning differences and physical challenges.

★ Try out employer and employee puppets to role-play an interview or explain how to fill out a job application.

★ Let food puppets teach about nutrition and good eating habits.

★ Use puppets of different shapes, sizes, and materials to help children compare, classify, and evaluate.

★ Construct puppets from the hands-on materials used in math, such as Unifix Cubes, tangrams, and attribute blocks. Use them to teach and reinforce math concepts.

★ Make a puppet from a ruler, money, or a clock and use it to teach math skills or to present math problems.

★ Create puppets in different shapes for a unit on geometry or fractions.

★ Use a puppet TV newscast to report world, local, and current news.

★ Explore or explain careers and occupations with puppets who are doctors, dentists, police officers, truck drivers—the list is a long one!

Learning with Puppets

Puppets don't have to be for the teacher only. Let your students get in on the act and create puppet shows of their own. Students can use puppets to present their ideas on many subjects. The following are some student-led puppet ideas:

★ Reenact history. Columbus, Vasco da Gama, the Pilgrims, Betsy Ross, Lewis and Clark, Chief Joseph, Jane Addams, Marie Curie, and Martin Luther King Jr. are just a few who would work well this way.

★ Practice problem solving by setting up a problem situation and then having the students work it out with puppets. Ask, "What's the problem, and how can it be resolved?" It's a good idea to set a time limit for this.

★ Use puppets to show ways to deal with stressful situations like tests, class presentations, or disagreements.

★ Encourage shy students to use puppets for sharing or show and tell. Students tend to open up more by "acting" through the puppets because it's the puppet doing the talking, not them.

★ Let students use an animal puppet to tell all the facts known about that animal.

★ Have a scientist puppet such as an archeologist or astronaut explain about his or her specialty.

* Make puppets from math manipulatives and let students use them to tell about math facts.

* Have students use puppets to tell stories in a foreign language they're learning.

* Encourage a group of students to prepare a puppet quiz show, newscast, or talk show on almost any subject. They could do a "Morning Report" (news, weather, and sports) using different puppets. (See the "WACKY News Script," pages 66–67 for a sample script.)

* Literature and puppets seem to have been made for each other. Use puppets to act out stories, poems, or jokes. Students could memorize them or a narrator could read as the students manipulate the puppets. They could perform scenes from fairy tales, books, or short stories they've read.

* Have kids try improvising stories or scenes from books with puppets. To improvise, the puppeteers should be assigned characters. They need to know the storyline, certain key phrases, the main points, and the ending. Then they can act out the rest, changing certain aspects of the story, or create funny stories by switching around the characters. For example, use a soft, mild voice for the villain or a huge, hairy puppet for the princess. The type of puppet to use in each story is usually self-evident.

* Let students write and perform their own stories with puppets they create.

* Use puppets to do interviews with characters from a story, an author, a scientist, a math whiz, a world traveler, or a person from another country.

* Play "Charades" with puppets. Kids can pantomime a word, an idea, a concept, or a phrase from almost any subject. This puppet activity will help them perfect their manipulation skills.

* Create a game called "Show Time" to give kids practice with puppet movements and speech. Give each show a specific theme such as dancing, singing, or telling jokes, riddles, or poems, and invite students to prepare a small act that fits with the theme and falls within a time limit. Have the skits include very active things such as the puppets running and chasing each other, falling down, falling in holes, crashing into each other, dancing fast and slow, dancing out of step, tripping, or flying.

Are You Sold on Puppets?

People of all ages enjoy puppets. Kermit the Frog and Miss Piggy have been guests on late night TV talk shows—and I doubt kindergartners were watching! Puppets are very useful tools in the classroom. They can enhance any subject. They work with both young children and older kids. Puppets can be cute, silly, and even sophisticated. Best of all, they can be fun!

Make Your Own Hand Puppet

Directions for Teachers & Students

1. Photocopy and cut out the pattern. Pin it to two layers of fabric or felt. Cut out along the heavy solid lines. (Copy image at 110 or 120 percent to increase size of pattern.)

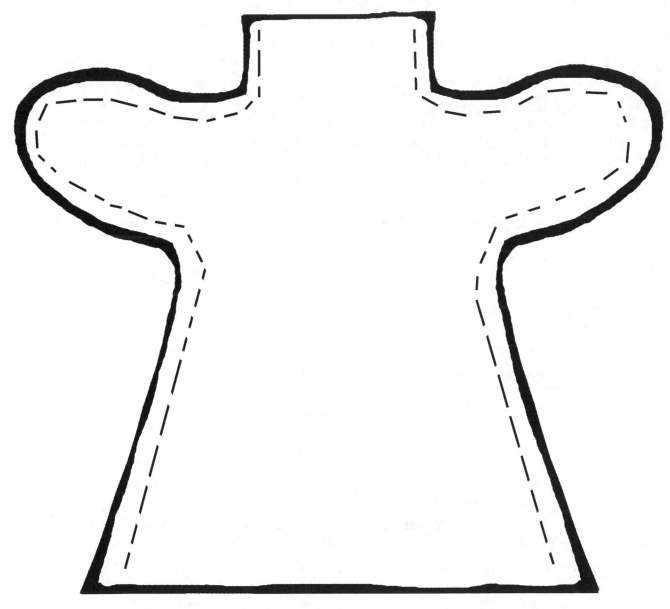

(MORE)

Make Your Own Hand Puppet (continued)

2. With right sides of the fabric together, stitch along the seam line (dotted line). Or use fabric glue to glue the pieces together. Leave the neck and bottom open.

3. Clip the curves, then turn body right side out.

4. Cut or punch a hole in a Styrofoam or rubber ball, large enough to fit over your index finger, for the head of the puppet. Paint or glue facial features on the ball. Add yarn hair, a hat, or whatever else you wish to the puppet head.

5. Place your hand inside the body piece and poke your index finger up through the neck hole. Attach the head by pushing on the ball.

PART 3

Laughing Through the Curriculum

THIS SECTION WILL GIVE YOU:

✓ ideas and suggestions for using humor in different subject areas
✓ help in creating new ideas for your curriculum.

Your curriculum will never be the same once you start using some of these ideas. Try them out. Move them around. What works in one area might also work in another.

Don't let the only time you get a smile out of your class be when you say, "Class dismissed." Humor can help make all subjects more enjoyable for more kids more of the time.

Reading & Writing & Laughing

Tips for Lightening Up Language Arts

"Laughter translates into any language."
—ANONYMOUS

The language arts offer many different avenues to explore using humor as your vehicle. You can read humorous stories, write comedies, spell funny words. The ideas and suggestions in this chapter are designed to help wake the humorous spirit in you and your students through reading and writing activities. You can teach the material as individual units or you can mix and match ideas. You might even want to use the ideas with other subjects. Activities such as a readers' theater or writers' exercises work just as well in science, math, or social studies. There are hundreds of humorous ways to teach language arts. Using sounds to teach punctuation, silly words to teach spelling, and cartoons to teach cause and effect are just a few. Work up some of your own ideas. Improvise! Put two things that don't seem to go together—together. See what happens.

Read 'em & Laugh!

Presenting a readers' theater is easier for children than performing plays. They don't have to memorize the lines and they don't have to "act." They can hold the script in their hands in full view of the audience. The audience is able to visualize the story because the narrator reads all the descriptions and thoughts. Many children's books can be written into readers' theater. Some, like the Morris and Boris books by Bernard Wiseman, the Amelia Bedelia books by Peggy Parrish, or the Arthur books by Marc Brown are easy to make into readers' theater scripts for early-elementary kids.

One way to adapt a story to fit a readers' theater is to simply take out the stuff between the direct dialogue. The following example from *The Wizard of Oz* illustrates how this type of script works.

Lion:	Roar.
Dorothy:	Don't you dare bite Toto!
Lion:	I'm sorry.
Dorothy:	You're nothing but a big bully.
Lion:	I know. I'd love to have some courage.
Tin Man:	The Wizard of Oz is going to give me a heart.
Scarecrow:	And he's going to give me a brain.
Dorothy:	Maybe you can come along with us and he can help you, too.

Reading the play and having the narrator fill in the "she said" or "he said" would be really confusing and boring:

Lion:	Roar.
Narrator:	Said the Lion.
Dorothy:	Don't you dare bite Toto!
Narrator:	Said Dorothy.
Lion:	I'm sorry.
Narrator:	Said the Lion.

Sometimes you have to use your discretion. The narrator might have to say, "She closed her eyes and opened her mouth wide and screamed." Or, "She covered the box with her shawl and sneaked away."

Here's the same scene written to include the narrator:

Narrator: As they traveled through the forest, a huge lion sprang at Toto.

Lion: Roar.

Dorothy: Don't you dare bite Toto!

Narrator: The lion hung his head in shame.

Lion: I'm sorry.

Dorothy: You're nothing but a big coward.

Lion: I know. I'd love to have some courage.

Tin Man: The Wizard of Oz is going to give me a heart.

Scarecrow: And he's going to give me a brain.

Dorothy: Maybe you can come along with us and he can help you, too.

Narrator: So the lion joined Dorothy, Toto, Scarecrow, and Tin Man. Soon the Yellow Brick Road led them to Emerald City.

Costuming for a readers' theater like this doesn't need to be elaborate. The actors might wear signs identifying them as Lion, Tin Man, Scarecrow, or Dorothy, or they could wear costumes, masks, or hats to say who they are. You could make signs look like huge nametags.

When selecting a story for readers' theater, try to choose one that doesn't have too much description and/or too many thoughts. Look for stories with a lot of direct dialogue. If necessary, revise or shorten a story to make it work. A very good readers' theater for older kids is Abbott and Costello's "Who's on First?" routine. You can find a print version of this routine in *Who's on First? Verbal and Visual Gems from the Films of Abbott & Costello* (New York: Darien House, 1972). Although this book is out of print, it should be available at your local public library.

All Together Now!

Choral reading is a little different from readers' theater. Everyone can read in unison, like a chorus, or one person can read, with groups of three or four people adding words or sounds.

Poems and very short stories are good choices to use for choral reading where the whole group reads in unison. It takes some practice to get the cadence together, but it can sound very good and sometimes it's very, very funny. If you've ever seen a Greek chorus you'll understand how this works. Mel Brooks, Woody Allen, and Spike Lee have all used this device in their movies.

It takes a little more practice if one person reads while groups add sounds. First, find a story where certain words are repeated often and can be associated with sounds: cat *(meow)*, dog *(woof, woof)*, train *(woo, woo)*. Assign groups of three or four students to each sound. Every time the narrator says the word, the group adds the sound. Here's how it works:

Words and Sounds:

alien: beep, beep, beep

spaceship: swoooosh!

stars: twinkle, twinkle

dust: achoo!

sun: hot, hot, hot

Once there was an alien *(beep, beep, beep)* flying in her spaceship *(swoooosh!)*. She flew to a star *(twinkle, twinkle)* to search for a friend. When the alien *(beep, beep, beep)* landed on the star *(twinkle, twinkle)*, all she found was a lot of dust *(achoo!)*. The alien *(beep, beep, beep)* jumped back into her spaceship *(swoooosh!)* and flew off to the sun *(hot, hot, hot)*.

You can expand the story, adding a new sound with each new character or object. Be creative, brainstorm places or things that have many different sounds, such as the circus, car or horse races, a farmyard, different forms of transportation, or a birthday party.

Playing Around with Plays

Here are a few short things to remember when writing humorous plays, readers' theater, or choral readings. Take a story and rewrite it without thinking about the number of characters and what is or isn't funny. Then revise it, adding, deleting, or combining characters until you come up with a workable number. The two key words in writing children's plays are *condense* and *delete*. When you come up with what you consider a workable play, you can start looking at what is or isn't funny. Add jokes, gags, or stunts. Look at the story from a different angle or viewpoint to come up with funny lines. For instance, in *The Wizard of Oz*, the lion could say to Dorothy, "You're an old meany weenie." His roar could be a meow, or he could have a squeaky voice.

Author! Author!

Another activity that will get your kids' creative juices flowing is an author study. Choose an author who is wild and funny and has written several books. Robert Munsch, Daniel Manus Pinkwater, and Dav Pilkey have written quite a few silly stories that early-elementary kids find really fun to read. For older kids, consider Beverly Cleary, Astrid Lindgren, E.B. White, or Louis Sachar. Some of their books and others are listed in "Really Fun Resources," pages 177–181. Invite kids to read as many of the chosen author's books as possible. Find out about the person's life. What motivates him or her to write funny stories? Encourage students to think of zany ideas that are appropriate to the book or author. Try some of the following "Fun Things to Do with a Book" for more ideas.

Fun Things to Do with a Book

★ When you read a book to the class, try reading with special emphasis on certain words or repetitive words. After awhile the kids will catch on and they'll say the words for you. For example, if the line, "Esmarelda said, 'Okay, okay, okay,'" is repeated throughout the story, after about the third time you can stop after, "Esmarelda said," and the kids will add, "Okay, okay, okay."

★ Have the students think of other repetitive phrases they, or their brothers or sisters, might have used as babies. "I don't want to." "Do I hafta?" "Mommy, Mommy, Mommy, Mommy, Mommy." "He pushed me." Can they write similar stories, using these new words or phrases? How about exchanging these new words or phrases with some in the author's story?

★ Choose a popular book and help the class turn it into a readers' theater, choral reading, or puppet play. Older kids could do it all themselves.

★ Have students re-illustrate a story using their own drawings or pictures cut from magazines.

★ Prepare one or more stories for a storytelling session. Invite students to pantomime the stories or use puppets to pantomime as you read them.

★ Have students create a comic strip or comic book on one or a series of stories.

Have kids try any or all of these book-related activities:

★ Many authors and illustrators use similar devices in every book. Pick an author or illustrator and look for similarities in all of the person's books. Are they intentional? How could you list or graph them?

★ Pick a favorite humorous author and write an imaginary biography of the person or one of his or her characters based on what you've read.

★ Combine two or more stories into one story. Make it as wacky as you want!

★ Write a newspaper headline and an article for a story. Be reporters on the scene of a favorite fairy tale. Interview the characters. Make it into a contemporary tale.

★ Turn a book into a TV script. Interrupt it with commercials.

★ Compose a story about a character from one story meeting a character from a different story.

★ Write a series of letters or email correspondence between people in different stories.

★ Write a diary for someone in the story.

★ Write a letter to the publisher of your favorite humorous book or stories. Tell them how much you enjoyed the humor in the book and what was funny about the book. Let the publisher know that you would like to read more books like the one you're writing to them about. Ask for a response back.

Single Subject Ideas

Choose a single topic that interests the majority of your class and do a series of projects that cross all subject areas. You could choose monsters, dragons, robots, fashion dolls, queens and princesses, kings and princes, toys, animals, cars, or any other topic the kids like. The list can go on and on.

Invite students to bring in pictures and examples of whatever topic you decide on. Make a large display of all the examples. Find both fiction and nonfiction books on the subject. Have the students brainstorm ideas. The following is an example to work from. It could be revised for any subject the class chooses.

Topic: Robots

- Create a book on robots. Do some research. Find out about the history of robots, different types of robots, unusual robots, robot songs, robot records, robot jokes, and robot poems.

- Design different types of robots.

- Create a simple robot (like a robot to take messages).

- Design and build robots from everyday items, such as detergent bottles, paper cups, and milk cartons. Motorize them by putting them on toy cars.

- Create robot games. Play them as if you were robots.

- Write robot stories. Brainstorm humorous ideas. Write stories as a group or individually.

- Design different uses for the robots you have.

- Make a robot from construction paper or tissue paper.

Really Fun Books

Fun books present information by using signs, recipes, laws, newscasts, weather, letters, and other intriguing methods. There are many such books on the market. For a listing of some, see "Really Fun Resources," pages 177–181. Encourage students to be aware of all forms of information (newspapers, Web sites, magazines, nonfiction books, television and radio news). Show them how they can use this information to make other types of books, including fun books. Use the "Make a Fold-Out Book" handout on page 105 to give kids one idea on how to present their stories.

Have the students make their own fun books by rewriting or retelling a story (or stories) using unusual methods. The following are some suggested ideas.

★ Write in the form of an autograph book of storybook characters:

"JILL PUSHED ME." —JACK

"Jill pushed me." —Humpty Dumpty

"Not me—not by the hair of my chinny, chin, chin." —Peter Pig

★ For older children, show them a copy of the Declaration of Independence. Ask students to write a few words about freedom or rights using a signer's style of handwriting. Can they also mimic the way people wrote back in the late 1700s, or the early 1800s? Have them compare *your* signature to John Hancock's.

★ A different twist on the autograph and handwriting activity is for your class to request autographs from their favorite authors, actors, athletes, or musicians. Help students research addresses or fan club information, and have them compose a short letter requesting an autograph and enclose a self-addressed stamped envelope.

★ Create a plot line using letters to and from storybook characters, historical figures, or contemporary people:

Little Red Riding Hood writes to the Three Little Pigs about the Wolf.

Captain John Smith writes to a tabloid magazine about exaggerating stories.

Betsy Ross writes to Martha Stewart about her design for the first U.S. flag.

Noah Webster writes to Will Smith about word usage and rhyming.

★ Write a story using letters of application for a job or résumés of storybook characters, historical figures, or contemporary people:

Little Boy Blue looks for farm work.

Goldilocks applies for a house-sitting position.

Amelia Bedelia looks for housecleaning jobs.

Florence Nightingale applies at a local doctor's office.

Artist Jackson Pollock looks for a summer job painting houses.

Elton John decides to tune pianos for a living.

★ Compose a story from the business letters of book characters:

Little Jack Horner writes a complaint to the pie company.

Jack B. Nimble complains to the candle company.

Alice writes a letter to the editor of the local newspaper complaining about the large holes throughout town that the city council has neglected to fill.

★ Use pager or answering machine messages from characters to create a new twist on the story:

"Jack, this is Jill. I just called to apologize. I didn't mean to fall."

"Dorothy—Glinda, the Good Witch, called in regard to the ruby slippers."

★ Create classified ads for book characters:

Wanted: Glue expert. Contact Mrs. Dumpty at castle.

Lost: Blue jacket in vicinity of Mr. McGregor's garden. Contact Mrs. Rabbit.

King needed. Must be able to work with wild things. Contact Max.

Looking for a meteorologist to forecast weather for the Dakota territories. Contact Laura.

Wanted for summer season only: Residential living in nice home, prefer two parents, no Dudley. Send message by owl to Harry Potter.

★ Write diary pages from different characters:

"Dear Diary, I wish my mom hadn't thrown out those beans tonight. I thought they were such a good deal. Maybe I can find them in the morning and plant them, or sell them, or even eat them. I wonder why Mom was so mad?"

★ Try writing fortune cookies or horoscopes for different characters:

"You are in for a great fall."

"Sleep well. You will meet the man of your dreams."

★ Put together a recipe book from different characters:

Wolf's stew—from Grandma's kitchen

Wolf's stew—Three Pigs style

Scrambled eggs a la All the King's Men

Grassland green salad—Laura Ingalls Wilder

★ Write up strange laws from different stories:

No more than four people living in one shoe.

Any person baking blackbirds in a pie will be prosecuted.

Any animal caught stealing from the pig's trough will be cobwebbed by Charlotte.

★ Compose headlines for different stories and then write up the account:

Wolf Attack Reported in Three Separate Incidents

House Break-in at Bear's Residence

New Diet Information from the Sprat Family

★ Put together a museum catalog of items presented by book characters:

Fox's tooth presented by Dr. De Soto.

Remains of straw and wood houses presented by two pigs.

One crystal shoe donated by Cinderella.

Hairpiece given by Rapunzel.

Wizard broom specialties from Hogwarts School.

Writing Exercises That Won't Cramp Your Style

Use the "Can't Think of Anything to Write?" handout on page 106 to help your students generate ideas of things to write about and formats to use. Make copies for each student or make a poster that lists just a few of the writing suggestions on it, then add more as the year goes on. Assign students to rewrite a story using items from your list. Here's a brief idea list using *Tuck Everlasting* by Natalie Babbitt (see page 179):

★ Signs:

Curved Road Ahead

No Hunting in Foster Forest

Keep Off the Lawn

Boat Rental

★ Business card for man in yellow suit

★ Newspaper headlines:

Child Abduction

Jail Break

★ News story about worried parents

★ News story of jail break

★ Interviews with family and sheriff

★ Classified ads:

> Wanted: Person to clean Tuck's house
>
> For Sale: Foster Forest
>
> For Sale: Very old Frog

★ Brochure for arts and crafts show

★ Recipe for pancakes

★ Letter to Ann Landers from Jesse

★ Contract between parents and man in yellow suit

★ Rules of jail

★ Menu at diner

★ Obituary

Easy as 1, 2, 3...

Ask students to write a how-to in ten steps or less. Encourage them to think of non-traditional how-tos. For example: how to make a bed without bumps, how to prepare for a test without complaining, how to survive school lunches, how to write a how-to. Read them out loud to the class and let the other students decide if the instructions are complete enough or if additional steps should be added to make the directions more clear.

It's a Group Thing

Here's a fun way to get budding authors to write. Let them do it as a group!

★ Form groups of three or four kids and assign each person in the group to write a story on the same theme or idea. Then let the students exchange ideas by reading their stories to the others in the group. After reading all the stories, have them write one group story, using the best parts of all the stories. When they're satisfied, invite the groups to read their finished products to the whole class. Or, let them present their stories to another class.

★ Use adding machine tape. One student begins writing a story on the tape. After writing a required number of sentences the student passes the story to another. The next person can read the whole thing or just enough to continue. (To make it interesting, roll up the paper so only the last sentence or the last two or three sentences are revealed.) The final story can be read and enjoyed, or critiqued and revamped.

★ The same idea can be done using a sheet of paper. The first student writes a starter idea on the paper and then bends the paper back so that only one or two sentences are shown. The next person picks up from there.

★ Let students work together to write a modern version of a fable or a fairy tale. Each group could work on a different story or the whole class could do the same one. You might also specify a particular author such as Hans Christian Andersen, the Brothers Grimm, Aesop, or even Mother Goose.

★ Have groups combine two or more fairy tales, fables, or rhymes.

★ Encourage groups to present their stories as a puppet show, comic strip, readers' theater, mask show (students create a mask for each character and perform the story—for more about masks, see page 152), or for storytelling. They could do their presentations to other classes or groups.

Shake & Bake

While I was searching around for new ways to present writing exercises to my elementary class, I remembered an idea from my cartooning days. Cartoonists and gag writers use a system of mixing and matching the names of people, places, and things to come up with humorous ideas. By placing normal people in strange settings with odd props, or by placing unusual people in normal settings, writers are able to come up with some pretty outrageous ideas.

I put together a collection of story "ingredients" that I call "Shake & Bake." You can use these story starters for writing exercises, puppet plays, readers' theater, storytelling, or any other activity that begs for creative ideas.

The recipe is very easy to follow. Label five separate containers, either small boxes or plastic food containers: (1) Sound, (2) Color/Pattern, (3) Covering, (4) Descriptive Adjective, (5) Body Part. Photocopy the reproducible chart "Shake & Bake #1" on page 107, and cut out the words. Place the words in the appropriate containers. (If you lightly color each category before you cut apart the words, it's easier to sort them later.) You can add or delete words in each category to make the lists appropriate for your class.

Have students pick at least one word from each category and use the words to write a description of an imaginary animal. Where does it live? What does it eat? What does it do? When students are done writing, have them draw a picture of the animal. It can be as strange as they want!

Once kids get used to working with the idea, you can expand on it. Use the "Shake & Bake #2" handout on page 108. Label the containers with the new categories, and have the students draw one or more slips from each.

Here's an example to show how the exercise works. Suppose a student draws these words: Scuba diver, desert, violin, fishing, weepy. He or she could make a sentence with them by adding some connecting words (that's permissible): *A scuba diver in the desert with a violin is weepy because he can't go fishing.* That's a good start, but why is the scuba diver in the desert? How did he get there? What's he doing with his violin? Is it all a mirage? Would he be saying, "I hope this is a mirage" or "Nobody will believe me back at the oasis" or "I've got to stop watching MTV"? The kids can take their stories in any direction they want!

Another way to use "Shake & Bake #2" is for students to pick a slip from the first category—people—and write a description of a character. Next they pick a place from category 2 and write a description of the place. Then they pick a prop, an activity, and an emotion and try to work them into a story. Help kids brainstorm by asking questions: Why is your character feeling this way when using this prop or doing this activity? Is there something else the character can do with the prop? Can she or he use it in a different way?

A quick starter is to have students write one paragraph describing the character, a second paragraph describing the place, a third telling the story, and a fourth ending it by bringing the story all together and making it interesting. Voilà—a complete short exercise in four paragraphs!

Another approach is to cut each category out so there are five separate lists. Put the lists next to each other and move them up or down until you find a match to use. Another method is to pick your own subject and then scan the lists for ideas that help. Students don't have to stick to the lists. Encourage them to use their imaginations, move words around, and add or delete until they come up with a "spark" of an idea.

Students could also cut out pictures from magazines and place them in appropriate bags or containers labeled: Hero, Antagonist, Setting, and Conflict. Have students draw from each bag and create a story using the pictures they selected.

Putting Some Punch into Punctuation

Kids make sounds all day long, intentionally or unintentionally. Some sounds are funny, some are annoying, and some are just plain disgusting. Use this to your advantage. Take a cue from Victor Borge and use sounds to punctuate sentences. (If you're not familiar with Victor Borge, you can check the comedy section of your local video store.) Have students make up sounds for periods, commas, semicolons, colons, question marks, exclamation points, and quotation marks. Assign different sounds to different students. Then have someone read a short piece while everyone adds their punctuation where they think it should go.

The sounds can be done with mouths, hands, or feet. They can be anything from whistles and claps to finger snaps and foot tapping. You could also try sound makers like snappers, horns, drums, whistles, and rhythm band instruments. Try different things. Let the kids decide which ones work the best.

How Do You Spell "News"?

Use newspapers or magazines to help teach spelling words. You can cut them out or mark them up. Try some of the following ideas with your class. Tell students to:

★ Copy down their spelling words and then search through magazines for each word on the list. When they find one, they can cut it out and paste it next to the word on the list.

★ Identify which spelling words are nouns, find a picture of each noun, cut it out, and paste it by the word on the list.

★ Identify which words are verbs. Find a picture of someone or something doing the word. Cut out the picture and paste it by the word.

★ Cut out letters from magazines to spell the spelling words. (When they paste them on the paper, it will probably look like a ransom note.)

★ Search for spelling words in a newspaper, and circle, underline, or draw a square around each word they find. How many times do they find the same word in the newspaper?

You might have students search for one word at a time. Give specific directions for what to do when they find each word. For example: circle the word *catch,* draw a square around *horse,* underline *bottle.* You can check to see if they followed directions correctly.

what Rhymes with Laugh?

Humorous poetry is a great way to add laughter to your day in small doses or over an extended period. Reading aloud a short humorous poem related to the topic before, during, or after the lesson, can help make the mind more receptive to other ideas. See "Poetry," pages 186–187, for a list of some poetry books with laugh-out-loud humor. The following is a short list of ways to add humor using poetry.

★ Collect or have kids collect a variety of poems on a single subject, such as dogs, cats, cars, sports, trees, siblings, school, or chewing gum. Present poems as a visual or verbal collage.

★ Have students illustrate favorite poems. They can combine all the elements into one picture, or illustrate each line or every two or three lines.

★ Make the poem into a comic strip.

★ Use pictures in magazines to illustrate poems.

★ Have puppets "read" some of the poems.

★ Let one person read the poem while others pantomime it.

★ Do a readers' theater poetry reading. For poems with no characters speaking, two or more students could read alternate lines. For poems with characters speaking, assign parts, including the narrator, to different students.

★ Present a choral reading. Read the whole poem as a group or divide the lines or characters among small groups.

★ Devise a rhythm or beat to accompany the poetry reading. Kids could clap hands, pat knees, snap fingers, or tap sticks together.

★ Write parodies of famous poems.

★ Add new verses to favorite poems.

★ Have students choose a word and then list all the words they can think of that rhyme with it. Write a class poem using the rhyming words.

★ Recite poetry and leave off a word. Let the kids fill in the missing word. For example:

Jack be nimble,

Jack be quick.

Jack jumped over

The candle _____.

Make it more challenging for older kids and leave out more words.

★ Find old nonsense poems. Have the students copy them or write their own renditions. For example:

Ladies and jellybeans, I come before you to stand behind you

to tell you of something I know nothing about.

Next Thursday, which will be Friday the 13th,

there will be a ladies meeting for men only.

Admission is free. Pay at the door.

Plenty of seats. Sit on the floor.

We will discuss the square corners of a round table.

When I read, I read reading.

When I write, I write writing.

But if I only wrote writing I wouldn't be able to read it

because I can't read writing.

So now when I write I write reading so I can read it.

See You in the Funny Papers

You can use cartoons with any subject, but they are especially useful in language arts. Can't find cartoons to fit your lessons? Create your own—the funnier the better! You don't have to be a great artist to draw cartoons. You can make them with the cut-and-paste method described in Chapter 10 ("Cut-&-Paste Cartoons," page 153). Or, use cartoons that your students draw. Some of them might be phenomenal!

Start a classroom cartoon collection. Cut out the comic strips that you like. Have kids bring in the strips that they like. Put them on a bulletin board or in a class folder. Remember when using published material you can only use it in its original form. With cartoons, you can cut them out, cut them up, paste them on something, or laminate them, but it's illegal to photocopy them.

Here are some ways to use comics in the classroom:

★ Have students put the strips in alphabetical order by titles or by author names.

★ White out or cover over word balloons. Have students write new dialogue.

★ Have students in groups or pairs take turns writing dialogue. Group 1 writes the first block, Group 2 writes the next, and so on.

★ Leave the word balloons in and cut off the last block of the comic strip. Invite students to write a new ending.

★ Give each student a few days of a comic strip with a continuing story line, such as "The Amazing Spider-Man," "Jump Start," or "For Better or for Worse," and have them complete the story.

★ Use three or four different strips. Cut each strip into separate blocks. Take a block from each strip and paste them together onto a piece of paper to form a new strip. For example, use one block from "Beetle Bailey," one block from "Hägar the Horrible," one block from "Doonesbury," and one block from "Blondie." Or you could use "Heart of the City," "One Big Happy," or "Garfield," or whatever is popular with your class. Then white out all the word balloons except the one in the first block. Let kids write new dialogue for the rest of the strip.

★ Have students write new captions for one-panel cartoons like "Dennis the Menace" or "The Family Circus."

Venn Are We Going to Do Venn Diagrams?

Compare and contrast different comic strips using Venn diagrams. What do the strips have in common? (Same number of panels? Same gender of characters? Same kind of pet?) What's unique to each? Or, compare and contrast people, places, or things in the same strip.

Use humor to reinforce alphabet learning. Draw a letter on the chalkboard, flip chart, or overhead. Make it into a person, an animal, or a thing. Do a couple to get kids started, then let them make their own. This is a perfect way to help kids with letter memorization. You could put two or three letters together to make a picture—and a word! This activity works with numbers, too.

Story Starters

Draw your own cartoon or funny action picture and display it for your class. Then have students try any or all of these ideas to get started on a story:

★ Describe the scene to someone who hasn't seen it.

★ Write down what happened before the picture, or what will happen next.

★ Write dialogue for the cartoon. Make it into a one-panel comic strip.

★ Make a list of particular things in the picture. What makes it funny?

★ Come up with a title, or several titles, for the cartoon.

Cartoons & Reading Comprehension

Use comics as a "shorthand" version to explain many reading comprehension skills: picking out details, identifying topic sentences, finding the main idea, cause and effect, making inferences, drawing conclusions, predicting outcomes, making generalizations, recognizing double meanings, and distinguishing fact from fiction or realism from fantasy. Search comic strips for examples of these skills to use in independent learning centers in your classroom. Clip the appropriate comics and laminate them for durability. Write questions for specific strips or a group of strips on 3" x 5" cards and put them in envelopes, along with the comic strips. Include questions like these:

★ "What caused Garfield to say or do that?"

★ "What does Dagwood mean when he says . . . ?"

★ "Is this fact or fiction?"

★ "What do you think will happen next?"

★ "What's the main idea of this strip?"

★ "What's the setting?"

Write the answers on the back of the cards for self-checking, or ask students to turn in their answers to you.

Vocabulary & Word Study

Cut out and laminate some popular comic strips and use them with kids to practice vocabulary skills: phonics, long and short vowels, consonants, blends, digraphs, diphthongs, root words, suffixes, prefixes, syllabication, compounds, rhyming words, synonyms, antonyms, nouns, verbs, and on and on. Students can:

★ underline, highlight, or make a list of words in a specific skill

★ list other words using root words, suffixes, or prefixes

★ list words that rhyme with a specified word

★ list words that are homonyms, antonyms, or synonyms for a specified word

★ replace nouns, verbs, and contractions with other words.

Sequencing

Comic strips are a great way to introduce sequencing. The strips are short and don't require a lot of prereading to get to the essentials. You can quickly present and model many different stories.

Most cartoonists use the same prop for a week or two or have recurring themes. For instance, "Garfield" uses a dish, a folding chair, and singing on the back fence. "Peanuts" uses a beanbag chair, a dog house, and a baseball field. These comic strips are good for sequencing activities. But look at other strips, too. Nearly all of them have recurring sequences of some sort.

To do the sequencing activity, laminate the comic strips and cut them into individual blocks. Arrange three or four days of one strip on the chalkboard ledge in no particular order. Work with the class to arrange them in logical order. They don't have to be assembled into original order. They just have to make sense.

Give some pointers to help students do the sequencing:

★ Explain that the artist signs a strip only once a day and the copyright appears only once a day.

★ Suggest that blocks can be sorted by items in the background, by items the characters are using, or by what the characters are saying.

With younger students, this works best as a group activity. What's most important is that they see the sequence and can understand or explain the story. Older or more advanced students could work on the sequencing individually. They might also write a paragraph describing the strip, including the setting, people, action, and dialogue.

Older kids might enjoy describing the story as if they were talking to someone on the phone. Or, they might have fun assembling into a logical order a combination of two or more strips that use the same prop or topic.

Punctuation & CAPITaLIZATION

Use cartoons to practice punctuation and capitalization by writing out or changing dialogue sentences in comic strips.

★ The dialogue of many comic strips is written in all capital letters. Have students rewrite it in sentence style.

★ Have students put everything that's in the talking balloons in quotation marks: "That's the correct answer," said Dolittle to the pup. "Now would you like to try the next one?"

Onomato-what-a?

Onomatopoeia. Words for sounds. Pow! Bam! Crack! Screech! Have students pick a few sound words and illustrate them or have them search for onomatopoeia words in comic strips or funny stories. Or, kids could write short plays that include sounds. Instead of making the sound, in the middle of the action students can hold up big signs with sound words printed on them. (Remember the old *Batman* television show?)

Not Your Average Book Reports

Are book reports becoming routine? Break the monotony by letting students do a book report on a comic book or turn a book report into a comic strip. Students can draw their own strips or work with a friend to illustrate the report. They can use stick figures or cut out figures from already printed cartoons. Or, they can use the computer to make animated reports. Software such as Kid Pix has slide show and animation options, and some Web sites for computer graphics offer free animated characters. See "Internet and Other Computer-Related Stuff," pages 193–194, for more information.

Don't Close the Book on Humor

These are just a few ideas of ways to incorporate humor into reading, writing, and spelling lessons. Scattered throughout this book are dozens more ideas you can use in the language arts classroom. Check them out, try some, and develop some of your own ideas. Enlist the help of your students, too. They'd love to get in on the fun!

Make a Fold-Out Book

A Project for Students

To make a fold-out book, you'll need several sheets of construction paper (all the same size), tape, and yarn.

1. Arrange the pages of construction paper in a row.

2. Tape the pages together along the edges of the paper.

3. Fold the pages together accordion-style.

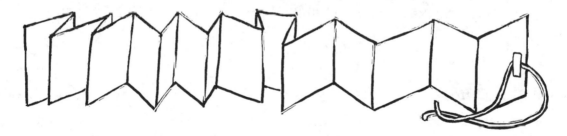

4. Cut a piece of yarn long enough to tie around the folded book pages.

5. Tape the piece of yarn to the back page of the book by placing the tape at the center of the yarn.

6. To keep the pages of the book together, tie the yarn at the front of the book.

Decorate your book however you'd like. You can write or paste in your story, draw your own pictures, or cut pictures from magazines, and add pockets or pop-up art to some pages.

Can't Think of Anything to Write?

66+ Ideas for Students & Teachers

ABC books	instructions	quotations
advertisements	interviews	raps
anecdotes	invitations	recipes
announcements	jingles	riddles
anonymous letters	jokes	road signs
billboards	journal entries	rules
book jackets	labels	shopping lists
brochures	limericks	signs
bumper stickers	lists	skits
business cards	memoirs	songs
calendars	memos	speeches
CD covers	menus	telephone books
chalkboard graffiti	monologues	thank-you notes
commercials	movie reviews	tongue twisters
contracts	myths	TV guides
diaries	news articles	want ads
dictionaries	notes	wanted posters
dreams	obituaries	Web homepages
editorials	parables	_____
fables	permission slips	_____
fairy tales	plays	_____
greeting cards	posters	_____
haiku	proverbs	_____
headlines	puzzles	_____

Shake & Bake #1

Story Ingredients for Teachers

Photocopy this page and cut out the words. Label five containers corresponding to the five columns below and place the cut-out words in their correct containers. Students can draw one word from each container and use those words to describe an imaginary animal.

1 Sound	2 Color/Pattern	3 Covering	4 Descriptive Adjective	5 Body Part
growling	yellow	skin	pointed	ears
squeaking	green	fur	jagged	eyes
beeping	blue	hair	dull	beak
clanging	red	feathers	long	snout
whining	purple	scales	short	nose
yowling	orange	fins	odd-shaped	bill
yapping	polka-dot	fuzz	sharp	horns
howling	striped	flesh	twisted	tongue
barking	spotted	crust	blunt	fangs
screeching	brown	grease	beveled	claws

Shake & Bake #2

More Story Ingredients for Teachers

Photocopy this page and cut out the words. Label five containers corresponding to the five columns below and place the cut-out words in their correct containers. Students can draw one word from each container and use those words to create a sentence.

1 People	2 Places	3 Props	4 Activities	5 Emotions
sailor	desert	computer	jumping	happy
artist	zoo	TV	playing	jealous
magician	dog show	armor	falling	surprised
dentist	bank	violin	flying	arrogant
hypnotist	spaceship	tombstone	camping	coy
doctor	North Pole	piano	sleeping	terrified
actor	airport	trombone	eating	sad
astronaut	ship	telephone	crawling	indifferent
plumber	airplane	umbrella	diving	curious
lawyer	bus	binoculars	digging	angry
monster	igloo	wig	painting	amused
scuba diver	shower	fireplace	sliding	mean
ghost	lighthouse	scissors	walking	overwhelmed

(MORE)

Shake & Bake #2 (continued)

1 People	2 Places	3 Props	4 Activities	5 Emotions
pirate	movies	telescope	watching	embarrassed
clown	barbershop	trash can	running	ecstatic
prisoner	flagpole	camera	climbing	proud
queen	subway	statue	acting	glum
king	moon	signs	fishing	weepy
cowpoke	school	toys	driving	disgusted
knight	elevator	newspaper	hopping	delirious
waiter	aquarium	bagpipes	counseling	cheerful
detective	museum	ice cubes	moving	disappointed
pilot	golf course	snow	hiding	irritated
opera star	laundry	drums	hunting	quiet
dancer	mine	glasses	swimming	distressed
chef	ocean	goldfish	dancing	delighted
jockey	cage	fish sticks	begging	dejected
baby	doghouse	balloons	calling	jolly
matador	escalator	stilts	buying	tired
elf	office	mask	inventing	afraid
barber	truck	horseshoe	drawing	contented
farmer	motorcycle	hammock	reading	ashamed
teacher	supermarket	totem pole	searching	blissful

Not-So-Serious Science

Science Experiments with an Element of Fun

"Humor can be dissected as a frog can,
but the thing dies in the process."
—E.B. WHITE

Science offers many opportunities to use humor in your classroom. The diverse subjects and themes and the demonstrations and hands-on activities are really ripe for humorous applications. Television has shown us this with *Mr. Wizard, Bill Nye the Science Guy,* and *Beakman's World.*

Humor and science are connected in many ways. Both employ imagination, creativity, brainstorming, problem solving, and logical thinking. Scientists and humorists find solutions in the same way. They connect things that weren't thought to be connectable. They find the unexpected. Surprise!

Toy Science

Add fun to a science lesson with toys. By examining and investigating toys, you can show students that science applies to everyday life. If you plan to use a toy to demonstrate a scientific principle, it's best to leave it out for a few days prior to the lesson. This way the students can play with the toy beforehand and they'll be better able to pay attention to the lesson when it's presented.

Toys can teach a number of scientific principles: motion, gravity, balance, pressure, heat, recycling, evaporation, inertia, sound, simple circuits, simple machines, liquid flow, circuitry, optics, and animals to name a few. For example, a kazoo can help demonstrate the concept of sound. A toy car or truck can show the principle of motion or illustrate a simple machine. When you look at a toy think, "What scientific principle can I teach with this?" Or, come at it from the opposite angle: "What toy can I use to teach this principle?"

Invite students to investigate a toy to find out everything they can about it. How does it work? What are its scientific principles? Let students formulate questions and design experiments that will prove or disprove their findings.

Recycling Cycles

Insert a little fun into a unit on recycling. Ask your kids to collect recyclable materials, such as cereal and detergent boxes, egg cartons, coffee cans, paper towel tubes, Styrofoam trays, and plastic bottles. Explain that reusing materials is one way to recycle. Challenge your students to create something new out of the materials. They could build monsters, robots, trucks, totem poles, and a number of other things from the junk material. Encourage them to use as many items as possible. String, beads, straws, or cotton balls can be added to enhance the creation. This activity can combine a few subject areas. For example, making a totem pole could integrate art with science (recycling), social studies (Native American culture), and reading (stories and poems about Native Americans). Making a monster could combine art, science (recycling), and language arts (storytelling).

For more ideas on recycling projects, check out some of the books in the "Math, Science, & Social Studies" and "Puppets" sections, pages 185–186 and page 187.

Also, look at the ecology in your area. See how the environment and the different habitats create an ecosystem for the plants and animals. Ask your students what they can create using the gifts nature has to offer. Beach glass washed along the shore is great for jewelry, tree bark makes an interesting picture frame, fallen branches are good for making a fort, and rocks and pebbles decorated with paint make colorful paperweights. What can your students create from nature in your area?

Sound Advice

The study of sound—how it's made, how it's transmitted, and how we receive it—offers many possibilities for fun projects. Making musical instruments is one of them. Sound is transmitted by vibrations. What better way to show this than with homemade musical instruments? Round up some scrap items and get to work. You can even make it a combined lesson on sound and recycling.

Try making these musical instruments with the class to illustrate different sounds:

★ Wrap different size rubber bands around a cigar box or shoe box for a guitar.

★ Fill bottles or glasses with water for a xylophone.

★ Glue two sheets of sandpaper onto 3" x 5" wood pieces to make sand blocks.

★ Seal beans, rice, or pebbles in plastic bottles or tin cans for simple maracas.

★ Invent your own instruments from the materials you have on hand.

Good Vibrations

Kazoos are a great instrument to use when teaching a unit on sound waves. When most kids first try to play a kazoo, they blow into it. They may be surprised to find that it makes no sound that way. Explain that you have to hum into the kazoo to get a sound. And what a funny sound it is! Once kids get used to the idea of humming, they'll really enjoy the kazoo.

Can't afford kazoos for the whole class? Make your own. For each kazoo, secure wax paper over the end of a toilet paper tube with a rubber band. Poke a hole or two in the top of the tube and start humming. You might have so much fun with the unit that you'll want to start a kazoo band. Find old wind instruments and use kazoos for the mouthpieces. A trombone and a kazoo could be a kazoobone or tromazoo. A trumpet and a kazoo could be a kazoopet or a trumpazoo. Try a bugle, a tuba, a clarinet.

Combine Art & Science

Really get creative and make all types of new musical instruments:

★ Flatten four or five metal bottle caps. Use a thick nail to punch a hole through the center of all of them. Thread them onto a thinner nail and nail them to a stick. (Don't pound the nail in too far. You want the bottle caps to be able to move.) They'll make a jingling noise as you bang or shake the stick.

★ Make a notch every few inches along a dowel. Rub another dowel against it to make a musical sound.

★ Rub rough sandpaper or metal screening with a stick to make a sound.

★ Use an aluminum or tin plate as a cymbal.

★ Hang kitchen utensils or pieces of metal from a cross bar on a stick to make a jingling sound.

★ Combine all of the above instruments into a one-of-a-kind music machine. Tape a can filled with dried beans to a broomstick, nail on some bottle caps, tack a pie plate on top, insert a dowel with dangling kitchen utensils, notch one side of the broomstick, and attach sandpaper to the other. Then bang, hit, scrape, and jiggle to make many musical sounds at once! Kids (and adults) love making and decorating these different types of musical sticks.

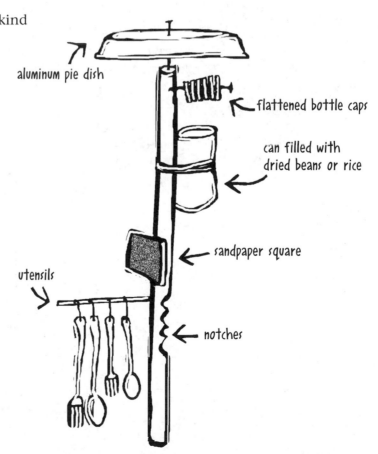

aluminum pie dish

flattened bottle caps

can filled with dried beans or rice

sandpaper square

utensils

notches

★ Cut two half-inch slits in one end of a paper drinking straw, then flatten that end and you have a whistle. Cut off the opposite end in short increments to get a deeper sound. You can change the sound by lengthening or shortening the straw, by punching holes in the straw, and/or by adding a paper cup to the end.

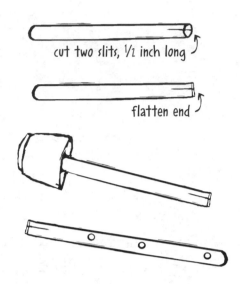

cut two slits, ½ inch long

flatten end

★ Blow in a garden hose or a funnel to make a unique sound. Put the funnel in one end of the hose and blow in the other end for a different sound. The length of the hose determines the sound (higher or lower). And twirling the hose over your head as you blow into the other end sounds like a whole bugle corps.

★ Cut off the top of a plastic soda bottle and use it like the funnel end of a trumpet or bugle. Screw it into one end of a hose (or tape it on with duct tape). Blow in the other end. Experiment with different size funnels and different size hoses—long, short, fat, skinny. How does the sound change?

★ Thread three feet of string through a hole in the bottom of a plastic or metal bucket, and secure it with a large knot inside or tie the string to a piece of wood inside the bucket. Hold the bucket upside down with your foot resting on the top of the bottom of the bucket, and pull the string up to about waist high and pluck it. The string will produce different sounds as you release or tighten the tension.

★ Start a jug band with soda bottles or half gallon or gallon containers. Different sizes produce different tones. Adding water will also change the sound.

★ Put together a rhythm band with a small group or the whole class. Start with everyone using the same size instrument (box, tub, bucket, can, tin, plastic, wood, cardboard). They can also use their desks as instruments by beating with their hands or sticks. Practice doing rhythms in unison. After mastering rhythms in unison, progress to two different size containers. Give half the group one size and half the group the other. Here's a simple rhythm to try:

Boom, boom, bam.

Boom, boom, bam.

Boom, boom, bam, bam.

Boom, boom, bam, bam.

Let the kids invent rhythm patterns of their own. For variety, add different sizes to make more instruments.

For more music and sound ideas and activities, check out *Rubber-Band Banjos and a Java Jive Bass* and *Sound FUNdamentals* (see page 186).

Loco-Motion

Demonstrate motion with toy cars or airplanes, balloons, balls, skates, tops, yo-yos, and Frisbees. Consider these moving science questions:

★ Have a contest. Which ball will roll the farthest? Does weight, size, texture, or surface matter? Can you design a way for a ball to go from one end of the classroom to the other without pushing it? Can you use eggs or other items instead?

★ What material makes the best spinning top? Does weight matter? Does size matter? Does surface matter?

★ What are some of the different ways you can make a toy car move? Gravity, spring and gears, air power—are there others? Can you find toy cars that use different methods to move? Can you make a car with no motor go up a slope? Can you design a car that's powered by a rubber band?

★ What principles are involved in yo-yos, Frisbees, hula hoops, and paddle balls?

★ How high can a ball bounce? Can you measure it? Does the size or shape of the ball affect the bounce? Does it bounce better on a hard or soft surface? Why do balls bounce?

Watching Water Work

It seems that nearly all kids are interested in water. They'll play in it or with it for hours. Use that to your advantage. Watch them to find out what they like doing. Then design science experiments around their play.

★ Consider what does and doesn't float. Does size, weight, or shape affect an object's ability to float? Find something that doesn't float and devise a way to make it float. Design something that helps a brick float.

★ Give each student a half-pound ball of clay. Demonstrate that the ball won't float. Challenge kids to design clay boats that will float, using all of the clay. Try adding weight to the boats. Which boats perform better? Why?

★ Examine puddles after a rainfall. Why do puddles form in certain places and not others? What is the biggest puddle you found? The smallest? How can puddles be measured? How long does it take a puddle to dry in the sun? When someone makes a splash in a small puddle, what type of a pattern does it leave? Have students draw that pattern.

★ Blow bubbles. What causes them? Is it the water, the air, the bubble "solution," the bubble wand? Is it possible to make bigger bubbles? Smaller ones? Square ones? What about star shapes or other shapes? Can anyone make long bubbles shaped like a tunnel? Different colored ones? Can people hold bubbles in their hands?

★ Take a small empty milk carton and punch a small hole in the lower right corner of every side. Punch a small hole in the top of the carton and hang it from a string through this hole. Fill the container with water. What happens? Why is it spinning? What causes it to spin? Devise other water activities like this.

★ Fill a one- or two-liter soda bottle to the top with water. Screw the cap on very tight. Stick a pushpin into one side close to the bottom and stick another pushpin into the opposite side. Pull out both pins at the same time. What happens? Why doesn't the water come out? Did it seal itself? What happens if someone squeezes the bottle? If someone takes off the cap?

★ Use four or five bottles of different sizes and shapes: tall and thin, short and fat. Fill each bottle with the same amount of water. Add different colors of food coloring to each to make it interesting. Have students arrange the bottles from the one that appears to hold the least amount of water to the one that appears to hold the most. Pour the water out into separate containers all the same size. Are the students surprised? Why do some bottles look like they hold more than others?

Stuck on Magnets

We've all done the experiment to see how many paper clips or pins in a row a magnet can pick up. Use the same principle, but cut out small paper acrobats or trapeze artists and put pins through or paper clips on them. How many can be hung from a magnet? Can students make them do tricks? If you can't make acrobats or trapeze artists small enough, cut out different colored pieces of paper the size of the paper clips or pins.

Here are some other magnet experiments:

★ Attach a magnet strip or button magnet to a small toy. Or, cut out a dancer or an ice-skater figure from paper and attach it to a magnet. Place the figures on a platform of lightweight cardboard or thin wood or plastic. Make the figures move by using a second magnet under the platform.

★ Clip a paper clip to the end of a piece of string. See if students can make it move like a snake by using a magnet in front of it, but not touching it. Can they make it rise off the table? Can they make it move with the magnet underneath, as in the previous idea? Have kids write a short play or story using these magnetic puppets as characters. Can they make them dance to music?

★ Spread metal filings onto a sheet of tagboard. Then have students move a magnet around underneath the sheet to draw pictures or write with the filings.

★ Make small plastic cars move by using magnets taped to them. Who can move them the farthest or the straightest? Is it easier to pull with the magnet, or to push? Is it easier using the magnet under a sheet of cardboard, or wood?

★ Make a fishing pole from a stick, string, and a small magnet. Use it to fish for items. What items won't it pick up? Ask your students to think of other ways to make it pick up these items.

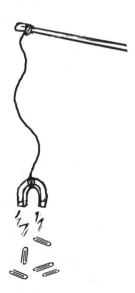

★ Investigate the variety of magnets available. There are many different shaped magnets on the market that you can use to show repelling and attracting. Magnets shaped like washers work well on a stick or a pencil. There are marble magnets and magnets in almost any shape imaginable.

Lend Me Your Air

These ideas are good for a unit on wind or air movement or flight:

★ Design vehicles that kids can move by blowing on them. Can students devise a way to get the air to the vehicle more efficiently? How far will the vehicle go on just one blow? What could make it go farther? Can it pull things? How much weight can it pull?

★ When you blow up a balloon and release it without tying it off, why does it go in a zigzag pattern? Who can devise a way to make it go in a straight path when it's released? Who can make it go in a circular path?

★ Invent or design different shaped paper airplanes, helicopters, or birds. What can be done to make them fly higher or farther?

Lite Light

A study of light offers some great opportunities to "lighten up" your lessons:

★ Use a flashlight, a gooseneck lamp, or an overhead projector to make shadows on the wall. Invite kids to make hand-shadow animals, like a dog, rabbit, bird, or swan. Where does a hand have to be to make the shadow? Where does the light have to be?

★ Cut out paper or cardboard figures to use for shadow puppets. Devise ways to make their arms or legs move. Write plays to use with the shadow puppets.

★ Try this activity outdoors on a sunny day. At what time of the day are shadows longer? How can students find this out? Ask kids questions like these: Can you make your shadow in front of you? Behind you? On the side? Can you make your arm disappear? Your leg? Your head? Use two or three bodies to make a monster shadow. Can you step on your partner's head? Can you devise some rules for shadow tag?

Simply Simple Machines

★ After an introduction to simple machines, present a mini-lesson on cartoonist and inventor Rube Goldberg who was best known for drawing and designing ridiculously complicated ways to do a simple job. His inventions would include numerous steps and hundreds of moving parts to accomplish the easiest task. The board game "Mouse Trap" is a good example of the kind of invention Rube Goldberg might develop. Have students devise a Rube Goldberg-type invention that uses all of the simple machines. Most encyclopedias will have information about him and pictures of him.

★ Invent and use products to do classroom jobs with simple machines.

★ Pick one simple machine and list all the possible uses for it. Also think of some uses that haven't yet been invented.

★ Identify what toys are made with simple machines.

★ Explore ways to make a wheeled toy go farther or faster.

★ Experiment with different things a lever can be used for.

Perfect Popcorn Popping Practice

Use popcorn to devise fun math and science projects. Consider this:

★ Pop corn in an air popper. While the popcorn is popping take off the cover. How far do the kernels go? Can the distance be graphed?

★ Research and discuss some of these intense popcorn questions (and any others that pop into your mind): What makes popcorn pop? Where does popcorn come from? Why are some kernels white and others yellow? Is a popcorn kernel a seed? What kind? Do the seeds taste like popcorn? If you cut a kernel in half will it still pop? What does it look like inside? Why do some seeds pop while others don't? Does popped corn weigh more or less than unpopped corn?

★ Make a funny popcorn prop by gluing strings of plastic popcorn (typically used as Christmas tree decorations) onto a rolling pin. Tell the kids it's popcorn on the cob. (Real popcorn can also be substituted in place of the imitation stuff.)

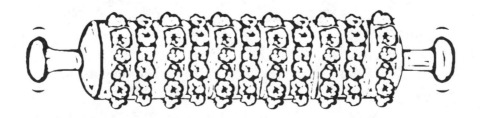

Go to the Head of the Classification

Collect sets of different things. Assorted rubber bands, rocks, keys, shells, bolts, nails, buttons, pencils, erasers, earrings—the list is endless. Use the items in classification exercises:

★ Have students sort the items by shape, size, color, or whatever classification system they choose. As they get better at it, have them classify the items into more and more categories.

★ Have students classify in categories they can noticeably measure, not just fat and skinny or big and little. How big is big? How fat is fat? An item that is brown, long, and rectangular, could also be light brown, six inches long, two inches wide, and have jagged edges. Another item in the same category could be tan, five inches long, one inch wide, and have smooth edges. Encourage students to make subcategories.

★ Challenge students to think of as many different categories as they can to classify an item. How many different ways can people in the classroom be classified?

★ Play "What's My Category?" Pick one or two ways to classify people in the classroom, such as by brown hair and glasses. Say, "Thanh and Anjali fit my category but Deandre doesn't." Students name themselves or other students who they think fit the category but without guessing or stating the category out loud. When enough students have been shown to fit or not fit the category, they can then guess what they think it is.

Body Part Art

A study of body parts can incorporate many of the arts, from poetry and music to dance and drama. Here are just a few ideas:

★ Make up poems, stories, or songs to name the different parts of the body. You can perform the following as a poem, a rap beat, or a chant by pointing to the parts and clapping when appropriate.

Cranium, mandible, clavicle, ribs.
Clap, clap, clap.
Clap your phalanges.
Humerus, radius, ulna, phalanges.
Clap, clap, clap.

Clap your phalanges.
Pelvis, femur, fibula, tibia.
Clap, clap, clap.
Clap your phalanges.

★ Photocopy the "Bone Up on Your Skeleton Knowledge!" handout on pages 124–126. Cut out the bones and assemble them as skeleton marionettes. Then put on a show. The answer key is below.

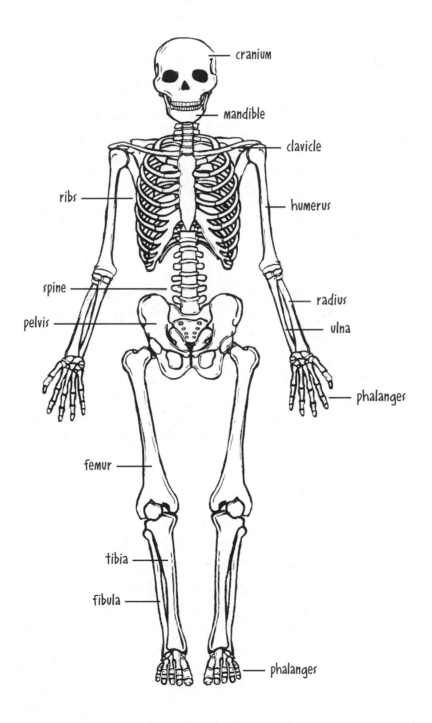

★ Make skeletons using recyclable material. Paint paper tubes white and attach them together. What else can you use to build a body?

★ Make up stories about how different body parts and organs got their names. Where did the name mandible come from? Liver? Phalanges? Kidney? Femur? Intestines? Ulna? Brain?

★ Place food or other items that could replicate a body part inside a box that has a hole for a hand to reach in. Have kids stick their hands inside the box and guess what "body part" they're feeling. Have them write down their answers. After the whole class has taken a turn, reveal what each "body part" is and what you used to replicate it. You can use cooked spaghetti for muscles, peeled grapes for eyeballs, dry corn kernels for teeth, gelatin for brains, or a balloon filled with oatmeal and coated with petroleum jelly for a heart.

★ Break the class into small groups and have the kids come up with their own ideas for "body parts." Have each group bring to class one or two of their ideas and see if they can stump the other groups.

Gross Goop, Mush, & Slime

Kids love gross stuff. Capitalize on their infatuation with crude, icky things by letting them create their own. Janice VanCleave has some great recipes in her book *200 Gooey, Slippery, Slimy, Weird, & Fun Experiments*. Besides all the gunky stuff, she also tells you how to make a fruit-fly trap and a volcano. Check out "Math, Science, & Social Studies," pages 185–186, for this and other stomach-turning and mucky books that kids will love.

Brainstorms.com and the *Things You Never Knew Existed* catalogs also have some great oozing, goopy, or weird things to use in science experiments. (See "Catalogs, pages 188–191.)

Science Art

Create space on your science bulletin board for cartoons, and encourage students to bring in science-related cartoons that they find. Have students classify which science category the cartoons fall into: plants, animals, humans, water, air, space, motion, sound—you get the idea.

Also invite students to create science art. They can make drawings of what a scientist is or what a scientist does. (Many will draw pictures of Dr. Frankenstein in his laboratory—encourage them to explore other ideas, too!) Or, they can make cartoon drawings of the animals your class is studying.

Science Puppets

What better way to introduce science subjects to young children than with puppets? Use an animal, bird, or insect puppet to teach about trees, weeds, plant life, ecology, and biology. An alien or astronaut puppet could teach about planets, space, rockets, weather, and many other subjects. See Chapter 6 "On with the Show!" for lots more ideas on using puppets in your classroom.

The Magic of Physics

Use the "Amazing Science Tricks!" handout on page 127 to liven up a science lesson. Your students might even put together a science magic show to present to other classes. Check out "Math, Science, & Social Studies," pages 185–186, for additional sources of science experiments.

Continue to Experiment...with Laughter

Science can seem so serious, but there's almost always a way to add a little humor. I hope the ideas presented here inspire you to experiment with ways to liven up your lessons. It's not feasible to list in one chapter all the ways to add humor. I've tried to highlight a few that have worked for me and that I think might help you jump-start your "humor batteries." Have fun!

Bone Up on Your Skeleton Knowledge!

A Body Part Puzzle for Students

Do you know which bone is which? Write the correct name on each body part. Then cut out the bones and assemble them into a complete skeleton. If you like, use a hole punch on each part and then put the parts together with paper fasteners to make a marionette.

cranium   humerus   spine   fibula

mandible   radius   pelvis   tibia

clavicle   ulna   femur   phalanges

ribs

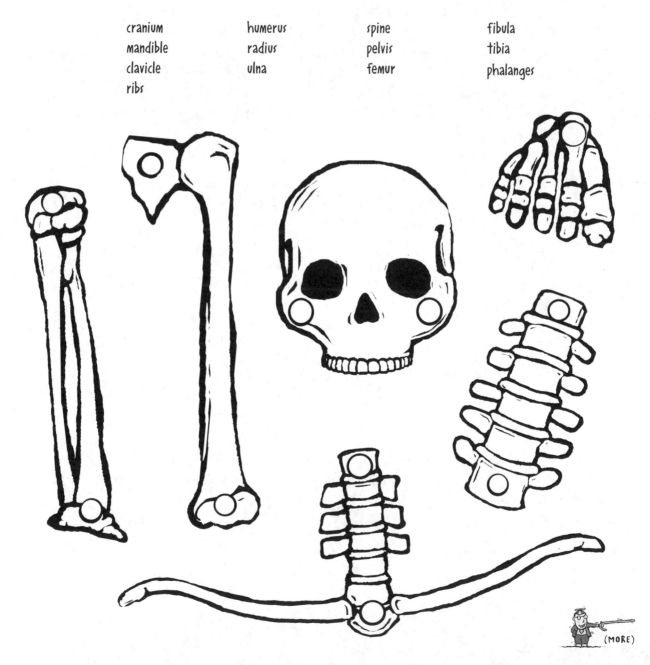

(MORE)

Bone Up on Your Skeleton Knowledge! (continued)

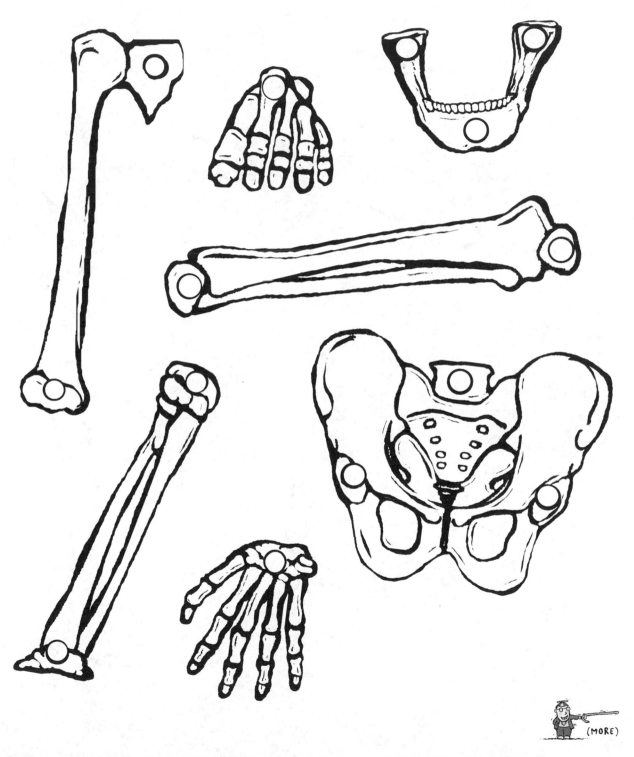

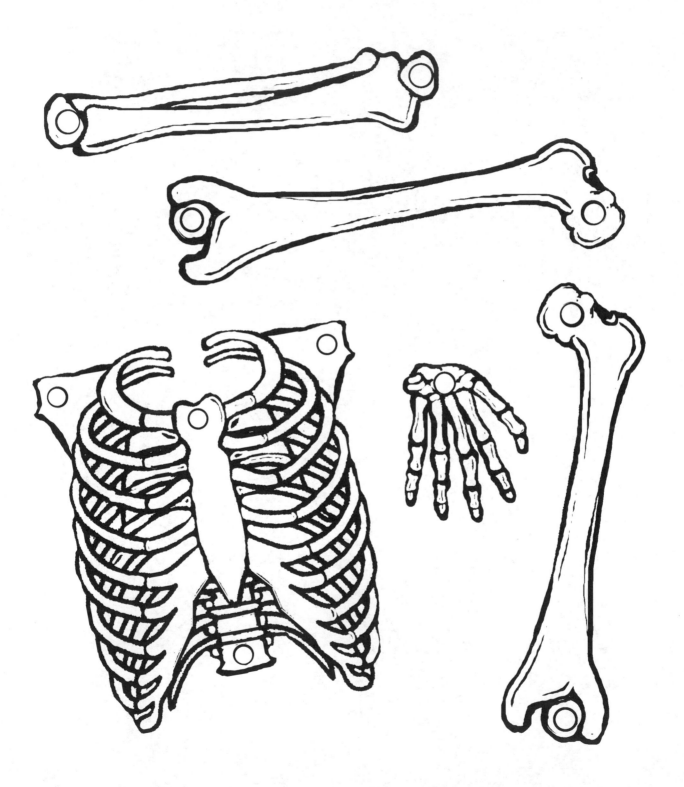

From *Laughing Lessons: 149⅔ Ways to Make Teaching and Learning Fun* by Ron Burgess copyright © 2000. Free Spirit Publishing Inc., Minneapolis, MN; 800/735-7323; *www.freespirit.com*. This page may be photocopied for individual, classroom, or group work only.

Amazing Science Tricks

Activities for Students

Make a Coin Dance

1. Wet the rim of a small, empty plastic bottle.

2. Wet one side of a coin.

3. Place the wet side of the coin on the rim of the bottle.

4. Hold the bottle tightly with your hand. Watch the coin dance!

wet rim

wet one side of coin

Test Centrifugal Force & Amaze Your Friends!

1. Hold a wire hanger as shown. Pull down.

2. Balance a penny as shown.

3. Using your index finger, swing the hanger gently back and forth, like a pendulum.

4. Twirl the pendulum faster in a full circle. The penny will stay on!

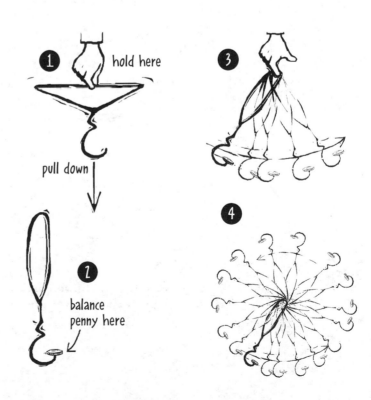

❶ hold here

pull down

❷ balance penny here

❸

❹

Math Mirth

Ways to Make Math Class Add Up to Fun!

"What do you do for a living?"

"I'm a mathematics teacher."

"Oh, yeah? Say something in mathematics."

"Pi r squared."

"You ain't so smart. Pie are not squared.
Pie are round. Corn bread are square."

—OLD BURLESQUE ROUTINE

Math, like any other subject, has great potential for excitement and fun. Just as you can find math in almost everything you do, you can find humor, too. You can add humor to practically any math lesson. The ideas in this chapter will show you how.

Adding, Subtracting, & Smiling

Addition and subtraction. The basics for all math. Kids have to learn these when they're young, and the work can be soooo repetitive. No wonder some kids have a tough time of it. Try subtracting a little of the routine from drills and adding some color, sound, and humor. The results will make you—and your students—smile.

★ Make or decorate the learning charts with colors or humorous pictures.

★ Use puppets, stuffed animals, cartoons, or kids' own funny drawings in place of the math book's buttons and beads. The math book asks, "How many buttons are on the coat?" Isn't it more fun to inquire, "How many puppets are lying down?" Or, "How many people are in that cartoon?" Or, "I have five stuffed teddies. If I take away three teddies, how many are left?"

★ "How many?" is a big question when you're learning to count. Make it fun for the kids by having them count things they know. "How many dolls are on the shelf?" "How many cars are on my desk?" "How many pieces of candy do I have in my hand?" "How many freckles do you have on your face?" (Have a mirror handy!)

★ Label boxes with numbers: 1, 2, 3 . . . up to 100 or whatever number you want. Have kids put that many toys, puppets, drawings, or gumballs in the boxes.

★ Make up sets of toys: four pop-up books, five bears, six balls, eight puppets. Ask children which set has four, or six, or whatever.

★ Let kids make their own number cards or a number book that goes up to ten. They can cut out funny pictures or cartoons for each number and paste them on. Or, they can draw their own pictures based on a specific theme: "My Alien Number Book," "My Clown Counting Book," or "My Weird Animal Book."

★ Tape number cards from 1 to 10 in random order on the floor. Don't space them too far apart. Challenge kids to hop from card to card in order without touching the floor. Try it counting by twos. Or hopping from odd number to odd number.

★ Put numbers on buckets or boxes scattered around the room. Invite kids to toss silly beanbags or fly paper airplanes into the containers, in order from 1 to 10, or backward from 10 to 1. They could also match items to the number on the container: throw four rubber noses or four plastic happy faces into the container marked 4.

★ Play a bouncing circle game. Have students sit in a circle. Give one child a ball and whisper a number to him or her. The child bounces the ball that number of times. Then the child rolls the ball to someone else. That person has to say how many times the ball was bounced.

★ For older kids, create unique word problems that use addition, subtraction, multiplication, and division. For example: I'm at the store to buy 36 cans of beans as treats for a party we are having at school. The store has four sealed cases of beans (each case has ten cans of beans) and one loose can. What's the easiest way for me to get 36 cans of beans?

Card Tricks

Play this game to reinforce addition skills:

1. Take an old set of playing cards. Write "Lose a turn" on all the face cards.

2. Divide the class into two teams. Make a column on the chalkboard for each team.

3. Draw a card and write that number in each team's column.

4. Explain the rules of play: The first player on Team 1 draws a card and writes that number under the number you wrote. She or he then adds the two together and writes the answer. If it's incorrect, that player's number and answer are both erased. The first player on Team 2 does the same thing. If a player draws a "Lose a turn" card, the other team takes a turn instead. Continue playing until one team reaches 100.

Check out the Web site "Card Trick Central" for hundreds of card tricks (see page 193). It has tricks for beginners, math tricks, memory tricks, sleight of hand tricks, and more. It also has a place where you can share your own card tricks.

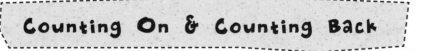

Counting On & Counting Back

Cut out characters from different comic strips. Paste together different characters on sheets of paper in groups of five, six, seven, eight, nine, and ten. Also have four loose individual characters.

Read this problem aloud: Five people were waiting for a bus (show a sheet with five characters). Dilbert and Beetle Bailey came to join them. How many were waiting for the bus? Students can use the cartoons to count on: five, six, seven.

Do the same thing with counting back. Nine people were sitting in the movie theater (show a sheet with nine characters). Four didn't like the movie and left. How many stayed to watch the movie? Count back. Say nine, then eight, seven, six, five.

Place a hula hoop on the floor or on a table and pretend it's a circus ring, a flying saucer, or a horse corral. Let kids count cartoon characters into it, or count back, removing characters as they do.

Double Your Pleasure, Double Your Fun

Remembering doubles of a number is helpful in learning math, especially mental math. Using rebuses or other representations as a mnemonic device can be extremely helpful and fun. The kids will enjoy using them and you can make some very funny wall displays from them.

★ *Double 2 is 4.* Use a picture or model of two bikes (two wheels each) or a wagon (four wheels) or a cartoon of a dog, horse, dragon, or any other four-legged animal.

★ *3 + 3 = 6.* Use a picture or model of two tricycles (three wheels each) or a bug with six legs.

★ *4 + 4 = 8.* Use a picture or model of a spider (eight legs), or a cartoon or picture of two four-legged animals.

★ *5 + 5 = 10.* Use a picture or model of hands or gloves.

★ *6 + 6 = 12.* Use an egg carton or a picture of a dozen eggs.

★ *7 + 7 = 14.* Highlight two weeks on a calendar.

★ *8 + 8 = 16.* Show two boxes of crayons (eight per box) or a picture or cartoon of two octopuses.

★ *9 + 9 = 18.* Display a nine of hearts and a nine of diamonds (playing cards).

★ *32 + 32 = 64.* Use two one-quart glass measuring cups with 32 ounces marked.

You could also use playing cards, dice, or dominoes for many doubles.

When you ask, "What is double fours?" the kids will remember the spider and eight legs. If they're doing a math problem and they can't remember eight plus eight, just mention boxes of crayons and they'll say 16. Rebuses and props can help them remember and laugh at the same time.

Edible Math

Use crackers, cookies, or candy to do math problems. Ask questions like these:

★ "Take two crackers and add two crackers. What do you have?" (Four crackers.) "Put peanut butter between them, and now what do you have?" (A sandwich!)

★ "If you had six cookies and you ate two, how many cookies would you have left?"

★ "How much is five M&M's and four M&M's?"

★ "How many pieces of candy are in this bag? Make an estimate and then count them. Were you close? What's the difference between your estimate and the actual number?" (Let them eat the difference, if it's not too large!)

★ "Look at the bags of candy. Are all the bags the same? How many more (or less) are in this bag?"

★ "Sort the pieces of candy in a bag by color. Multiply the total of one color by the total of another color. What's your answer? Or, if you had five bags of candy just like this one, how many pieces of each color would you have? What if you had ten bags?"

Counting & Exercise Fun

This is an idea for using exercise along with counting practice. Young children love it because they get to move. Older kids enjoy the silliness of it.

Count aloud as you touch parts of your body. Use opposite hands to touch opposite sides:

1—right hand on left foot	11—right hand on left elbow
2—left hand on right foot	12—left hand on right elbow
3—right hand on left ankle	13—right hand on left wrist
4—left hand on right ankle	14—left hand on right wrist
5—right hand on left knee	15—right hand on left hand
6—left hand on right knee	16—left hand on right hand
7—right hand on left hip	17—right hand on left ear
8—left hand on right hip	18—left hand on right ear
9—right hand on left shoulder	19—right hand on left eye
10—left hand on right shoulder	20—left hand on right eye

Then reverse and go back down. Do it faster each time. Alternate doing it fast, then slow. Do just odd numbers. Do even numbers. Try adding more parts: nose 21, mouth 22, chin 23, head 24.

Talk About Numbers

Pick a number. What are all the things you know about that number? The number three is a good one to start with. What can you associate with three? Three little pigs, three bears, three billy goats gruff, three men in a tub, three wishes, three strikes and you're out, three blind mice, three coins in the fountain (an old song that probably only I know), tricycle, triangle, trilogy, three stooges, triceratops, tripod, triplets . . . you get the idea.

Charting & Graphing Chuckles

You don't have to use just plain old boring lines and dots when charting and graphing exercises in math. Liven up charts and graphs with cartoons or pictures cut from magazines.

★ Make points on a graph into happy faces, fruits, different kinds of balls (basketball, soccer, baseball), planets, animals, coins, hands, doughnuts, or paper clips.

★ Turn lines or bars into snakes, rulers, pencils, buildings, books, people, boxes, sports sticks, or a hundred other things.

★ Think of odd or unusual things to use when teaching charting and graphing. How many (balloons, skateboards, soda bottles, soccer balls, math books, hats) will fit in a (box, bag, closet, can, car)? How many different colors? How many different sizes? How many different shapes?

★ Graph or chart favorite things (TV shows, movies, games, toys, colors, foods, fast-food restaurants, sports, sayings, sizes, clothes, books).

★ Graph or chart all of the attributes used on each newspaper comics page. How many squares, circles, or rectangles are used?

★ Graph the number of people or things in each comic strip or on each page.

★ On a given day, chart how many comic strips have one panel, two, three, or four. Chart this for a week or longer. Which day has the most panels? The least?

Merry Measurement

Who says measurement has to be done with standard measuring devices? What could you use instead of yardsticks, beakers, inches, yards, centimeters, millimeters, pints, quarts, or liters? How about using:

★ string—small pieces, long pieces, a whole roll, or shoelaces?

★ your hand, foot, or body?

★ other parts of your body, like your arm from elbow to wrist, or knee to foot?

What else could you use? Would these be a standard measurement? Could you make them standard? You could use things that are always the same size for a measuring device. Things like paper clips, boxes, spoons, eyeglasses, notebooks, desktops would work to measure things. Be creative. What else could you use? How about a teddy bear, a computer mouse, Matchbox cars, or Beanie Babies?

Increase the Volume...of Laughter

What could you use to measure volume? Avoid using things that are already marked with volume content, such as store bottles. Plastic containers, tin cans, coffee cups, and vases all hold liquid, but what about more unique containers? Plastic bags, balloons, hard hats, and camping coolers will all hold liquid, too. Can they be used to measure volume? Challenge students to estimate volume and then come up with ways to measure it accurately. Kids will have great fun finding out how much toothpaste is in a tube!

Comical Measurement

When presenting a lesson on measurement, include some measuring tools that are out of the ordinary. Saying "This box is four spoons wide" may spark more interest than "This box is eighteen inches wide." "This container holds three hats full of water" is more fun than "This container holds three liters of water." Learning with a chuckle, a giggle, or a laugh helps students remember more easily. It also makes the day a lot brighter for you and the class. Try some of these measurement activities:

★ Measure the size of different containers. Measure their three dimensions. Compare the measurements of the different containers. Use a standard ruler, a metric ruler, and other measuring tools.

★ What size would a container be if it were doubled? Tripled? What could it hold? How could you measure cylinder containers?

★ What's the area of a tin, box, basket, file cabinet, desk, room (a room is a large container—it's filled with students)?

Silly Math word Problems

Why are some math problems so boring? Consider this problem: "Felicia has 33 blocks. Austen has 14 blocks. Nina has 6 blocks. How many blocks do they have altogether?" Who cares?!

Simply making the names and items silly or goofy might help pique interest in solving the problem. Here's an idea: "Zelda has 33 xylophones. Moigatroid has 14 maracas. Esmerelda has 6 electric guitars. How many instruments do they have altogether?"

That's a little funnier. But how about getting even goofier? You could alter the problem this way: "Bertha Beezleheimer has 33 whatchamacallits. Archibald Zoolegger has 14 thingamajigs. Hilda Honawinkle has 6 whozamabobs. How many things do they have altogether?"

Alterations like adding silly names or changing what's being measured, counted, or graphed can make word problems more interesting and less painful. Instead of apples and oranges, how about kumquats and kiwis? Instead of beans and tomatoes, how about asparagus spears and beets? Instead of dogs and cats, how about snakes, lizards, gorillas, or dragons? The kids will yuck it up.

More ways to Use Those Comic Strips

Look for comic strips with numbers in them. For example, find a character doing a math problem or handling money. Or look for a scene with a clock in the background. Then work a math problem around those things. Here are some sample problems:

★ If the clock behind Dagwood's desk says 10:30, what time will it be in 20 minutes? If Dagwood came in at 8:00, how long has he been at work? How much time does he have before lunch at 11:15?

★ Dennis the Menace has 35 cents. If you gave him 12 cents more, how much would he have? If he spent eight cents, how much would he have?

★ Charlie Brown's math problem is 816 + 342. What is the answer? Estimate if the answer is bigger than one thousand or less than one thousand. Are these one-digit numbers?

Number Crunching

★ Use numbers to draw a funny picture. Turn a number into a person's or an animal's head. (See page 101 for examples.)

★ Draw numbers in sand.

★ Make numbers out of odd things like straws, nails, screws, pennies, or pencils.

★ Twist your body into the shape of a number.

★ Have two people make a two-digit number with their bodies, or three people make a three-digit number.

Timely Lessons

Get the kids interested in time by showing and using different timepieces: sand clocks, sundials, cuckoo clocks, pendulum clocks, moving-eye clocks, water clocks. There's even a clock on the market that runs backward, for people who are losing time. Did I miss any? (You can find novelty clocks in *The Lighter Side* and *Things You Never Knew Existed* catalogs, see pages 190 and 191.) Have your class make and use their own clocks. Decorate the clock faces in your room. Take an old clock apart to see how it works.

Cool Calculations

Kids as young as first graders enjoy using calculators. Once they have a basic understanding of the different functions, you can combine spelling with math to add even more fun to their learning.

★ Have the kids punch in the number 7714. Tell them to turn their calculators upside down. Ask them what they see. You'll probably hear a lot of wows and giggles. Most will get it right away. A few will need a little coaching. (The word is *hill* if you don't have a calculator handy.)

★ Have the class decide which numbers equal which letters. 1 = i or l, 3 = E, 4 = h, 5 = S, 6 = g, 7 = L, 8 = B, 0 = D or O.

★ Have students write words or sentences by punching in a number and then turning the calculator upside down to read a word. The number 5514 upside down is *hiss*. 7718 is *bill*. 3504 is *hose*.

★ You can make many words with the letters: i, E, h, S, g, l, L, B, D, O. For example, some S words you can make are: *see* (335), *sob* (805), *she* (345), *SOS* (303). Try writing *slob*, *soil*, *sill*, *sell*, *shoe*, *sore*, *sigh*, *slog*, *side*, *sped*, *shell*, *shill*, *slide*, *speed*, *siege*, and *sleigh*. One thing kids will figure out is that they can't write a word that ends in D or O because that becomes the first number. You can't punch in 0335 for *seed*. The zero before a number is automatically dropped by the calculator.

★ Give kids numbers to punch in for words. Then use addition and subtraction to write words. For older kids you could use multiplication and division. Start with simple math:

What's 200 + 135? What's the word? *See.*

What's 930 – 125? What's the word? *Sob.*

What's 23 x 15? What's the word? *She.*

★ Have students make up riddles using calculator answers. When they get good at using two simple operations, go to three or four different operations:

What did the snake say to the rabbit? The answer is 2,054 plus 3,460. *(Hiss.)*

What has a tongue and eyes but it's not your face? The answer is 5,862 minus 2,817. *(Shoe.)*

What would you call someone who ate everyone's lunch? Multiply 254 by 3, add 249, and subtract 407. *(Hog.)*

What do your parents have that birds carry around with them? The answer is 2,864 multiplied by 25, minus 15,532, plus 1,650. *(Bills.)*

★ You could also tell stories using numbers and the kids could add up all the big numbers:

I got in the space rocket and blasted off to the planet's moon 238,857 miles away. When I got to the moon I circled it for 124,510 miles. I landed safely on the moon. 13,249 space creatures greeted me and made me _____. (376,616 upside down is *giggle*.)

★ For more calculator fun, photocopy the handout, "Teacher, Is This Spelling or Math?" on page 143 to use with your class.

Time for a Technology Upgrade?

A funny idea to use with each new class is to introduce the first calculator that you used in school. Cut five finger holes in a small piece of cardboard or plywood. Poke your fingers through. Demonstrate how you calculated math problems with this "advanced" piece of technology.

You could do the same thing with a computer. Bring out an apple to introduce the first "apple" computer. Tie a pair of chattering teeth (from a novelty shop) to the apple for mega "bytes" or bring out a butterfly net to represent the Internet. You can use many ideas like this to get a smile, a laugh, or even a groan!

Gee, I Like Geometry

Use comic strips to show or practice perimeter, area, volume, and symmetry. Focus on each individual strip, a set of strips, part of a page, or a full page. You can also use cartoon characters and comic strips to show symmetry and congruency.

★ Which characters or strips are symmetrical or congruent? Which are not?

★ Which strips have square panels? Rectangular? Circular?

★ What shape is the "Dennis the Menace" strip? The "Cathy" strip? "The Family Circus" strip?

Fractured Fractions

Fractions can be tricky for kids. Help them get into fractions by using tangible, but unusual, examples.

★ Use real food for learning fractions. Divide up that pie! (And eat it, too?)

★ Break a cracker or cookie into quarters. Show the comparison of one-fourth to a whole.

★ Use clay or blocks of Styrofoam that you can chop into parts.

★ Look at comic strips as fractions. Which strips are divided into halves, fourths, thirds, sixths? Divide different panels or strips into these fractions.

Math Magic

Magic is a good way to add humor to a math lesson. Almost all tricks using cards, coins, counting with numbers, and dice will help in one way or another to teach a variety of mathematical concepts.

You should be able to find many books on math magic at your local library or bookstore. Check out the ones written especially for children. Start with books on cards or money. Look for connections to concepts you're teaching.

Here are a couple of math tricks to try with your class:

Trick #1: Sponge Balls. Use four one-inch sponge balls that you can buy at a magic shop. Put two balls in your right-hand pocket. Conceal one ball by squeezing it in your right palm with your last three fingers. Hold the other ball between your thumb and first finger. Ask, "How many balls do I have in my hand?" They'll say one (you hope).

Squeeze that ball into your right hand, along with the other concealed ball, being careful not to reveal the one already in your hand. Say the magic word, "Mathracadabra!" and blow on your closed hand. Ask, "Now how many do I have? One?" Show the two balls.

Then say, "Let's put one of these balls away. Put your hand with the two balls into your right-hand pocket. Squeeze the two balls together and pick up a third ball from your pocket between your thumb and finger. When you pull your hand out of your pocket, show only the ball between your thumb and finger. Ask, "How many do I have now?" Then repeat your magic word, blow on your hand, and reveal the two hidden balls.

Do the trick one more time, picking up the fourth ball in your pocket. Repeat the magic word, blow on your hand, and reveal all four balls. You can add more balls, or a larger one, or a square one.

If you go to a magic store, the salespeople will gladly demonstrate this trick before you buy the sponge balls. Once you see the trick done, you'll realize how simple it is! All it takes is a little practice.

Trick #2: Addition Magic. Write the following numbers on a piece of 8½" x 11" poster-board with a marking pen, just as they're written below.

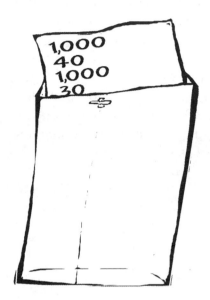

```
1,000
40
1,000
30
1,000
20
1,000
10
───────
4,100
```

Put the poster into a 9" x 12" manila envelope. Be sure you can easily pull the poster from the envelope.

Begin the trick by pulling the poster up just far enough to reveal the first number: 1,000. Ask students to say what that number is. Explain that you are going to pull the poster out of the envelope one number at a time. What you want them to do is add the new number to the old number and call out the answer. As you pull up the next number (40), the kids should say, "One thousand forty."

Next they'll say, "Two thousand forty."

Then, "Two thousand seventy."

Then, "Three thousand seventy."

Then, "Three thousand ninety."

Then, "Four thousand ninety."

Finally, "Five thousand."

Ask them to repeat the last number. "Five thousand."

Draw out the last number to reveal the real answer: 4,100.

Try it. It works every time. Your brain and your eyes play a trick on you. It's a good way to teach that we have to be absolutely positive about our answers. Don't always take the first answer. Check and recheck. Prove your answers.

Step Away from the Book!

There's no rule that says you have to rely solely on your math textbook. Many books contain some very clever ideas for presenting math, such as Anno Mitumasa's *Anno's Math Games* or *Anno's Counting Book* and David Schwartz and Steven Kellogg's *How Much Is a Million?* Margaret Kenda and Phyllis S. Williams's *Math Wizardry for Kids* is a good source for fun and challenging math puzzles, games, and projects for kids up to sixth grade. (See "Math, Science, & Social Studies," pages 185–186, for more information.) You can also find some very creative games and puzzles at specialty stores for kids, parents, and teachers such as Noodle Kidoodle. Look around, try out some different things, and liven up math class!

Teacher, Is This Spelling or Math?

A Calculator Quiz for Students

Use your calculator to answer the questions. What words are made from the following numbers?

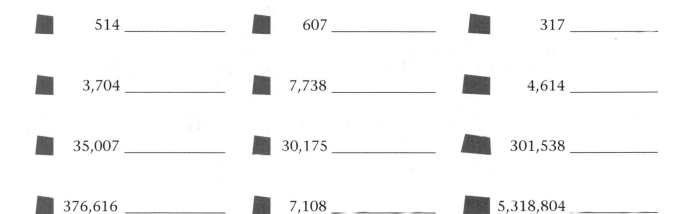

■ 514 _____   ■ 607 _____   ■ 317 _____

■ 3,704 _____   ■ 7,738 _____   ■ 4,614 _____

■ 35,007 _____   ■ 30,175 _____   ■ 301,538 _____

■ 376,616 _____   ■ 7,108 _____   ■ 5,318,804 _____

What numbers do you need to make the following words? Experiment to find the answers.

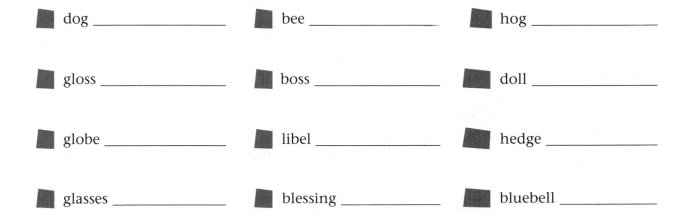

■ dog _____   ■ bee _____   ■ hog _____

■ gloss _____   ■ boss _____   ■ doll _____

■ globe _____   ■ libel _____   ■ hedge _____

■ glasses _____   ■ blessing _____   ■ bluebell _____

The Muse Is Loose

Laughing Through Music & Art

"If I didn't start painting, I would have raised chickens."
—GRANDMA MOSES

Music and art can add humor and enjoyment to any classroom, and new dimensions to many of the activities already mentioned in this book. Look for ways to use art and music to accentuate or add to ideas that you try. Of course, you can include creative arts as a simple background to any lesson, but try to go a little deeper than that and make them a central part of the learning activity.

The following ideas include ways to integrate art and music into different subject areas and to use the arts by themselves to provide humor in the classroom.

Let's Have Some Music!

Music in the classroom can help brighten the mood and bring a festive atmosphere to all your learning. Sing or play CDs, tapes, records, or instruments to bring music into the classroom daily. You can even make your own instruments. Use the instructions in Chapter 8 (pages 112–115) to create a classroom band.

In the Mood...for Learning

In the background, play instrumental music without voices. Vocal music will be distracting, and songs that kids know the words to will probably have them singing along. Sing-alongs and dancing have their place in a classroom, but not necessarily during a math or science lesson.

Try a variety of recorded music—classical, jazz, pop, world, or folk for background music. Play music that uses different instruments—guitar, piano, accordion, harpsichord, dulcimer, bagpipes, or full orchestra.

The Grand Entrance!

Play entrance music as students enter the room to get them pepped up for the day:

★ vaudeville music

★ circus preludes

★ marches

★ polkas

★ Dixieland jazz

★ opening themes to TV shows

★ tunes associated with various cartoon shows

★ Hollywood fanfares or movie overtures (trumpets and bugles and gladiators)

Use different types of music to introduce particular subjects or themes.

Make It Festive

For a festive atmosphere try a variety of international music from Poland, France, Italy, Spain, Africa, or the Middle East. Music from other cultures also is a perfect fit for social studies units.

★ Play recordings of unusual instruments like the accordion, bagpipes, sitar, marimba, steel drums, African drums, or an Arabic aud, rebab, and dumbac.

★ Try carousel music.

★ Play a recording of old-time player piano music.

★ Put on calliope music.

You can order many of these recordings and instruments through catalogs. *Music K–8 Marketplace* is a good source of unusual musical resources. Their catalog lists a variety of collections of songs, along with videos and music recordings of many different instruments from around the world. (See page 190 for more information.)

Sing It Out

Sing out your instructions even if you don't think you have a singing voice. The kids are sure to find the instructions (and your singing) entertaining:

★ Try an operatic, "It's time to take out your reading books!"

★ Sing instructions to the tunes of old or new songs: "Let's sit up and do our work, e-i-e-i-o."

★ Use different voices, volumes, and tempos.

Encourage the kids to sing, too:

★ With younger children, use songs to teach the alphabet and counting.

★ Older kids can learn songs from history or history from songs.

★ Use songs to teach foreign languages and learn about different cultures.

★ Learn all the official state songs, or at least your own.

So You Want to Lead the Band!

Play classical music, marches, big band songs, or jazz recordings and invite individuals or the whole class to "conduct." This is a way of getting kids interested in a variety of music. Pick a day and invite students to bring to class a musical instrument that they play. Have students give a brief demonstration of the instrument and maybe play a short song for the class.

Jump Notes

Teach whole, half, and quarter notes with movement games. Put on appropriate music, clear a space, and let the kids move around the room. This exercise will help to teach them musical notes, coordination, rhythm, and possibly even dancing. You could even incorporate the game into your study of fractions in math.

★ Quarter notes are *little step, little step, little step, little step* for 4/4 time and *little step, little step, little step* for 3/4 time.

★ Half notes are *big step, big step.*

★ Whole notes are *jump* or *leap,* depending on how much room you have or how much movement you want.

★ *Hop, walk, walk—hop, walk, walk* will really help the kids remember 3/4 time.

★ Incorporate dance steps with the rhythm and invent your own line dance. Call out the beats as the music plays, and take steps to the right, then left, or forward and backward. Have the students follow your lead.

★ You can also have kids practice rhythms while sitting down and clapping hands.

Wacky Recordings

Use humorous recordings to add humor to your day. You can find children's recordings that teach everything in the curriculum. Raffi is one of the big names for young children, but there are many other artists to choose from.

And don't just use children's recordings. Try some funny old songs, too. Dr. Demento has recorded many of the old crazy songs on CDs and tapes, such as "Purple People Eater,"

"Monster Mash," and "Witch Doctor." You might also check out recordings by Weird Al Yankovic and Ray Stevens. Ask students for their suggestions of current or new music that might fit into the "wacky" category.

Silly Song Games

Use songs the kids know to make up song games. Students could either sing the answers or say them.

★ Sing or play a line from a song or jingle and let kids supply the next line or word. They don't have to get it right. It might be funnier if they don't!

"On top of spaghetti . . ."

"I'm a little teapot, short and stout. Here is my handle . . ."

"I wish I were an Oscar Mayer wiener . . ."

"M-I-C-K-E-Y . . ."

★ Divide into teams and find out who knows the whole song for:

"Down by the Bay"

"Frosty, the Snowman"

"The Hokey Pokey"

"Take Me Out to the Ballpark"

Check out the book *Gonna Sing My Head Off!* (page 186) for more song ideas.

★ Challenge students to sing or say a song that has one of the following items in it: a color, an animal, a number, or a fruit or vegetable.

★ Give students a word and have them make a list of songs that contain that word. For example: feather, red, bird, up, little, happy, a person's name—the list can go on and on.

★ Have kids write parodies (new words to old tunes). Here are a few suggestions to get the kids started:

"Frère Jacques" (or "Are You Sleeping?")

"Oh, Do You Know the Muffin Man?"

"Twinkle, Twinkle Little Star"

"London Bridge Is Falling Down"

"Polly Wolly Doodle"

"She'll Be Coming Round the Mountain"

"Row, Row, Row Your Boat"

"Jingle Bells"

"If You're Happy and You Know It"

"This Old Man"

"Three Blind Mice"

"The Farmer in the Dell"

"Old MacDonald Had a Farm"

"B-I-N-G-O"

"The Old Gray Mare"

"Yankee Doodle"

"Here We Go 'Round the Mulberry Bush"

The Art of Humor

Art is a part of everything in a classroom, from lessons to decorations. Most, if not all, of the things in this book involve art. You can put a smile on someone's face with a mask, a costume, a puppet, a sign, or any of the other things talked about in this book. Sometimes humor is in the artwork, but most of the time art just adds to our enjoyment or defines the humor. Art helps us to look at things differently and shows us how other people look at things. Which is basically where humor comes from—looking at things differently.

A Hodgepodge of Humorous Art

Use collages and montages to create artistic masterpieces. A collage is made with various pieces of materials such as paper, wood, or cloth glued on a surface. A montage combines several separate pictures into one composite picture. Collages or montages can be created for any subject:

★ words and sentences for language arts

★ people and places for social studies

★ collections of numbers or sets for math

★ animals, environments, tools, machines, or any number of other things for science.

Encourage kids to make their creations fun. Who says art is limited to flat pieces of construction paper? Try these ideas for a more interesting project:

★ Glue collages to the sides of boxes and pile them up to make a class tower.

★ Cover three-ring binders or notebook covers with pictures that represent the different subjects.

★ Create three-dimensional collages or montages on a bulletin board.

★ Make a class portrait using montage. Let kids cut out bodies from paper, cardboard, cloth, magazine pictures, or whatever. Encourage them to portray themselves doing something they enjoy (playing ball, dancing, reading, or being a superhero). Use individual class pictures for the heads. Make it as funny as you can.

Draw Me a Picture

Find clever ways for kids to create drawings, either as an art project or as a quick transition activity. Emphasize the fun part. Let the kids know that the drawings don't need to look professionally done. They're not painting the Sistine Chapel.

★ Cut out full-page faces from magazines. Cut the faces in half, from top to bottom, or through the center of the face, from left to right. Glue one half of the face on a piece of paper. Invite the student to draw the missing half.

★ Have students draw with their nondominant hand.

★ Try drawing a picture without lifting the pencil off the paper.

★ Draw a design on the board with straight lines, squiggles, dots, or circles and squares. Have the students copy it. Start with a simple design, and as students get better at it, add more lines.

★ Have students draw designs from spoken instructions: "Draw a circle in the upper right-hand corner of the paper. Draw a triangle that touches three sides of the paper."

★ Show some caricatures and talk about what makes them funny. If you know someone who does caricatures, invite the person to visit your class. Let kids try drawing caricatures of their own.

★ Photocopy various famous paintings (it's legal to make photocopies of art as long as the copies are used only in the classroom). Let students turn the famous work of art into their own humor piece of art. Provide additional paper, crayons, markers, scissors, and magazines, so the students can draw or add to the copy of the painting however they'd like. Or, let students trace or sketch the work of art and then adapt it however they'd like. Display the new creations around the room to create your class's very own art museum.

Step-by-Step Art

Use the handout, "Step-by-Step Art" on pages 156–157 to complete this activity. Make a copy of the page for each student. Tell students to follow the steps to make a figure cut from paper and then to write directions for making a duplicate. Students will exchange directions and try to make their classmate's picture from the directions.

You'll be surprised at how well kids can do this activity. When you compare both drawings and the instructions, it's amazing how close many of these creations are. I've done this successfully with classes as young as second grade. Many skills are involved in the completion of this project—giving and following instructions, placement, measurement, sequence, relationship, and identifying size, shape, and color.

Color Me Funny

Color is sometimes a significant feature of a piece of art. But colors represent a variety of things or feelings for people around the world and during different eras. For example, in western nations, brides traditionally wear white at their wedding. Brides in China, however, wouldn't wear white, because in China white symbolizes mourning. During the

Middle Ages, the color brown stood for mourning, but today in western nations, black is the color that represents mourning. Green is sometimes considered a peaceful or restful color and red sometimes represents danger or anger. Ask students what the different colors represent to them. What color do they associate with humor or fun? Have students draw something humorous using primarily their "humor" color.

who was That Masked Man?

Design and make paper masks, crowns, or hats to add a little pizzazz to a variety of subjects. Use them as room decorations or for special days, or make them just for fun.

★ Make animal masks in science, reading, or social studies.

★ Create different hats or crowns to use when studying different cultures or countries in social studies.

★ Research how masks have been used throughout history. How are they used around the world? Design masks for holidays and other special emphases: Halloween, Mardi Gras, holiday plays, or units on other people and cultures.

Layer Your walls with Laughs

Add humor to the signs, posters, and windows in your classroom even if it's only taping on a funny picture or cartoon. Or, display some of these creative projects:

★ Come up with a funny class logo or mascot. Let kids paint posters using the image.

★ Let kids vote on a fun name for your class and then design pennants or flags from felt, fabric, or paper.

★ Have each child design a personal "coat of arms" on a poster board shape. (Don't forget the arms!) Hang them on a clothesline across your room or along the hallway.

★ Paint pictures on your windows with tempera paint. You could do a series of pictures on a theme or create a storyline.

Trophies

Have students create humorous trophies to be used as awards at informal awards ceremonies. The trophies could be made of paper or plastic cups, wooden or plastic railings, bleach or detergent bottles, plastic dolls or action figures. Let imaginations run wild.

Cartoon Capers

Cartooning is a very popular art form for kids of all ages. Cartoons seem to be everywhere—in comic books, magazines, newspapers, greeting cards, advertisements, movies—even an entire network on cable TV! Capitalize on the popularity of cartoons and use them in your teaching. See Chapter 7, pages 99–104, for more ideas on using cartoons and comic strips in the classroom.

Funny Faces

Use the "Make a Face!" handout on page 158 with kids as an exercise in creating cartoon expressions. Give each student a copy of the page. As you call out a variety of expressions, have them add eyebrows and mouths to the pictures. Use these expressions (in whatever order you wish):

happy	scared	furious	stressed out
sad	tense	ecstatic	calm
angry	sleepy	mean	lively
bored	surprised	hungry	goofy

Cut-&-Paste Cartoons

Cut out pictures from magazines or greeting cards. Some pictures will be funny, but they don't have to be. Cut off the head, body, or limbs of several different figures, mix them up, and then glue them together. Arrange different pictures together to make funny scenes. Have the kids use cutout pictures to illustrate their stories or lessons.

Art Olympics

Do this project during field days or as a year-end project. Let groups from the same class or different classes compete against each other.

★ Ask each student to bring in all kinds of recyclable junk—cereal boxes, foam trays, craft sticks, plastic spray can tops, paper towel tubes, plastic bottles—in a large paper grocery bag. After collecting the students' junk, place all of it in one pile in the middle of the work space.

★ Form teams of three to six people. Give each team a roll of masking tape and some construction paper. Explain that on your signal, they're to begin building a creation using only the recyclable junk and the materials you have given them.

★ Keep the rules simple. The winner's the group that builds the highest creation within the time limit or until all the materials have been used. Groups aren't allowed to hoard the materials; a person can only take one item from the junk pile at a time, and can only return to the junk pile after the first item has been attached to the group's creation.

★ Set a time limit of 15 to 30 minutes to complete the project. Give time checks or countdowns of minutes left to go.

★ The winner is the group with the tallest creation when time (or materials) runs out. You can also give other awards such as sturdiest creation, most colorful creation, quietest group, group that argued the least, and so on.

Take a Seat

For this 3-D art activity, you'll have to collect corrugated cardboard boxes ahead of time, and cut them into rectangular and square pieces of various sizes. Divide your class into groups of two to four people. Students are to use the pieces of cardboard to construct a chair that is able to support the weight of one person. Before the class begins the activity, discuss with them the definition of a "chair."

Students can use scissors, rulers, pencils, and any amount of cardboard. Notching and gluing is also allowed.

Award the group who successfully completes the activity first. Give each group an award for categories like: smallest chair, simplest design, tallest chair, most clever creation, fanciest chair, most sturdy chair, chair most likely not to be sat on.

Humor Is a FINE Art!

Incorporate music and art into other subjects. Use the ideas from this chapter to help get you started. Then combine them with other ideas, expand on them, add some new twists, experiment, brainstorm. Think of ways to get the kids to laugh or chuckle or just grin. Keep an eye open for ideas that will get your kids interested, involved, and smiling.

Step-by-Step Art

Directions for Students

Create a picture. Then tell a friend how to do it. Follow the directions below:

STEP 1: Tear or cut out a picture (like a monster, robot, truck, airplane, skyscraper— whatever you want to make) from pieces of colored construction paper. Make it a simple design, one that someone else could easily copy.

STEP 2: Paste your creation onto a separate sheet of paper.

STEP 3: Write step-by-step instructions in the instructions box so that someone can make a picture just like yours. Include the size, shape, color, and location of the things in your picture. Be as specific as you can.

STEP 4: Exchange this instruction sheet with a friend. But don't let the other person see your picture!

STEP 5: Now make a new picture from the instructions you have received from your friend. How does it compare with your friend's original picture? How does your friend's picture compare with yours?

(MORE)

SIZE:

SHAPE:

COLOR:

DETAILS:

Make a Face!

An Activity for Students

Add eyebrows and mouths to the faces below to show the variety of emotions and expressions that your teacher will list for you.

11

Phizz Ed & Games
for the Hall of Phame

Using Creative Movement
& Games in the Classroom

*"It has always seemed to me that hearty laughter is a good
way to jog internally without having to go outdoors."*
—Norman Cousins

Every teacher knows that children need movement. They squirm, they twitch, they bounce, they tap, they can't sit still. From kindergarten to graduate school, stored up energy seems to release itself in the classroom. It doesn't matter how old the students are. But by using creative movement and games coupled with humor, you can corral some of that energy to stimulate imagination and learning.

The exercises and games in this chapter will help students to relax and make them more open to expressing themselves. These ideas will help the shy and timid students as well as the outgoing kids. Educational research has found that students have many different learning styles. Students with a kinetic (motion) learning style usually benefit from a motion activity before a lesson. The motion activity helps to get them on track.

Whenever you look out at your class and notice that you're losing them (their eyes are glazed over, they're looking everywhere but where they're suppose to, they're one step away from snoring), it's time for a little break. You could have them stand up and stretch and then get back to work. But it might be more beneficial—and a lot more fun—to take a five minute humorous activity break. Both the kids and you would appreciate it.

Turn on the Tunes

Music is an excellent way to get the students motivated. Take a short break in the middle of the afternoon when attention spans start to decrease and play some music. Allow the kids to get up and perform their own interpretation of the music. Each day play a different style of music: rap, country, classical, rock, alternative, Latin, polka. Invite kids to bring in their own selections (be sure to preview the song before playing it for the whole class). Let the kids portray the melody and mood of the music through their dance moves.

The Human Pretzel

Crossovers are a great way to get the blood flowing and the giggles going. To do the basic crossover, move your right arm across your body to the left side while moving your left leg across your body to the right. Then switch. Move your left arm across your body to the right and your right leg across your body to the left. When done in rhythm this looks like marching. It can also be done to music.

A variation is the *cross touch*. Touch your left knee with your right hand. Then touch your right heel in back with your left hand. Do a few times then reverse. You can also do this by touching your left knee with your right hand, then touching your left heel with your right hand. Try alternating them.

Now you can try *sitting crossovers*. Touch your left knee with your right elbow. Touch your right knee with your left elbow. Touch your left toe with your right hand. Touch your right toe with your left hand. You can do this either sitting or standing.

Try doing crossovers with the eyes closed. For children having a hard time, place matching color stickers on coordinated body parts, for example, red dots on right hand and left foot; yellow dots on left hand and right foot.

Sitting Aerobics

Pick four or five of the following movements and do four repetitions. Then change the pattern.

★ Raise right arm (left arm; both arms).

★ Touch your shoulder with one hand (other hand; both hands).

★ Touch your head with your right hand (left hand; both hands).

★ Raise one shoulder (other shoulder; both shoulders).

★ Raise one foot (other foot; both feet).

★ Shake one hand (other hand; both hands).

★ Shake one foot (other foot; both feet).

★ Snap your fingers once.

★ Clap your hands.

★ Tap your desk.

Two-Hand Exercises

Warning: These coordination exercises will produce laughter!

★ Pat your head with one hand and rub your tummy with the other. Reverse hands.

★ Make a square in the air in front of you with one hand and make a circle in the air with the other.

The secret that I've found for both of these is getting one hand going first and then concentrating on the other. Try it. Some other way might work better for you.

Limber Fingers

Kids complaining of writer's cramp? Try these flexible finger exercises:

★ Form a V by putting your index and second finger together and ring finger and little finger together. (For *Star Trek* fans, this is the Vulcan "live long and prosper" salute.)

★ Next reverse the fingers. Put your second finger and ring finger together and pull the two outside fingers away from the center.

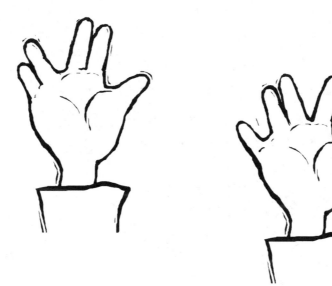

★ Try moving from one position to next and back again. See how fast you can change positions. Try changing hands. Do it with one hand and then the other. Try both hands together.

walk About

This is my personal favorite activity break. Have the children walk around your room without touching one another and quietly enough so they can hear your commands. As they walk, call out different objects or attitudes for them to mimic. Doing this three times a day can really change students' dispositions and get them back on track.

Invite students to walk around:

happy	big	sideways
sad	small	backward
mad	tall	with toes facing out
crying	short	with toes facing in
lost	tiny	on tiptoes
slow	huge	on heels
fast (without running)	waving	marching

Or, walk around like a:

dog	chicken	car
cat	robot	motorcycle
bear	square	question mark
monkey	circle	cloud
elephant	rectangle	big balloon
bunny	triangle	bowl of Jell-O

Here are still more ideas. Walk around:

with one hand on their head

with both hands on their head

with their hands over their mouth

with their hands on their shoulders

with their hands on their knees

like they're walking on marshmallows or eggs or marbles

like they're walking barefoot on a hot sidewalk

like they're skipping rope

This exercise can also include the statue command. Call out "Statues!" and the children have to freeze in whatever position they're in.

Mirror Image

Invite your children to face you and to mimic your movements, as if they are looking in a mirror. Move slowly at first. Move your hand or jaw, nod or shake your head, open and close your mouth or eyes. When they get the hang of it, pair them up and let them take turns leading and being the mirror.

Imagine That!

Walk around the classroom with a broom or yardstick. Hand it to someone, and tell him or her to turn the stick into an imaginary object and to demonstrate its use to the class. The class will try to guess what the object is. The stick could be a Pogo stick, a golf club, an oar, a broom, a horn, a magic wand, a stick horse—anything but a weapon. Explain that no swords, guns, or bows and arrows are allowed.

Try the activity with a variety of objects: cups, balls, pencils, a piece of cloth, or whatever else you have available in the classroom.

What Am I?

Ask students to pretend they are a certain thing. How would they act if they were an accordion, an elastic band, a wrist watch, a worm, a fish, popcorn, a jack-in-the-box, an escalator, an elevator, cooking food, a melting ice-cream cone, a swing, a pencil sharpener, a seesaw, a roller coaster, a Ferris wheel, a bottle of ketchup, a sprinkler?

Encourage students to move around to show what they are pretending to be.

Sound Memory

Blindfold one person at a time and take each through an obstacle course using sounds. Start with four sounds. The sounds could be snaps, whistles, claps, clicks, bells, horns, or any other single sound. Explain that each sound means to move in a different direction. For example, suppose the four sounds are clap, finger snap, bell ring, foot stomp:

★ On the first sound *(clap)* move one step forward.

★ On the second sound *(snap)* move one step back.

★ On the third sound *(ding)* move one step to the right.

★ On the fourth sound *(stomp)* move one step left.

Lead the students with a series of sound commands: *Clap, clap, clap* (three steps forward), *ding, ding* (two steps right), *clap, clap* (two more steps forward), *stomp, stomp, stomp* (three steps left), *snap* (one step back), *stomp* (one more step left), *clap* (one last step forward).

When they get better at it you can add more sounds and steps.

★ On the fifth sound make a quarter turn right.

★ On the sixth sound make a quarter turn left.

★ On the seventh sound make a half turn.

★ On the eighth sound sit down.

Quick Change Artist

Tell your students to carefully observe you as you stand in front of them. Explain that you are going to change one thing and they have to guess what it is. Leave the room or go behind a panel and change one thing: remove something (glasses, pencil from pocket, barrette), move something from one side to the other, mess up your hair, put on glasses, switch your tie. Return to face the class and ask them to guess what you changed.

Then tell them that you're going to change two things. Work up to changing four or five things. Don't change items back.

Another version of this activity is to have a group of three to four students stand in front of the class. The other students are to list any similarities among the group (all wearing glasses, all are the same height, all wearing jeans, all have similar shoes) on a sheet of paper. They shouldn't discuss their list with anyone else. Tell the students standing in front to go out to the hallway and change one thing about their appearance and then return to the front of the room. The class, as a team, should guess what changed and decide whether the group still has the same features.

Let Me Introduce Myself

Form a circle with your students. Explain that they'll go around the circle introducing themselves. The first student should say his or her name and add something that he or she likes along with an action that represents that thing. For example, "Hi, my name is Andre and I like pizza." *(Twirl hand like spinning a pizza or pretend to eat.)* The next person in the circle repeats what the first student said and did: "Hi. His name is Andre and he likes pizza. *(Twirl hand.)* My name is Annika and I like movies." *(Turn movie camera handle.)* Continue around the circle, with each person repeating what the person next to him or her said and did.

You can make it more challenging by repeating all the names and actions. Let kids help out with the remembering.

Line Ups

Have students form a line—WITHOUT TALKING. Explain that anyone who talks or even whispers must sit down. Students may use motions or body language but they can't speak. Call out a direction such as, "Line up by height, tallest to shortest." The kids will usually figure out that they can measure back to back and move around to get in the right order. For younger students, start with five or six kids. As they catch on add more kids.

Once students get really good at forming a line by height, change the request. Have them line up alphabetically by first or last name. Have them line up by birthdays. It may take them a while, but someone is sure to be ingenious enough to start holding up fingers for months or days or find a calendar and point out dates to each other.

Count Up & Count Down

Form a group of no more than ten students. Have students stand in a circle and count to a given number, but only one person at a time says a number. Start out with a low number, for example, have them count to five. Only one person speaks at a time. If two people speak at the same time, the group starts over. No one can say anything except a number. As they catch on to the game, add another rule: everyone must have his or her eyes closed. As they improve add more people or higher numbers. Or, count backward or by multiples of three or five or seven. How quickly can the group count?

Wheel of Fortune

Play this game based on the popular TV game show.

★ To prepare, choose several words or phrases from a current topic the class is studying. Photocopy the handout, "Wheel of Fortune," on page 173. Cut out the cards, and place them face down on a desk.

★ Form two teams. As host, tell how many letters are in the word and draw that many lines on the chalkboard. For example, if the word is *humor,* put five lines on the board.

★ The first player on one team draws a card and guesses a consonant. If the guess is correct, award that team the amount of "funny munny" on the card multiplied by the number of times that consonant occurs in the puzzle. Then pass the play to the next team. If the guess is incorrect or the player draws a "Lose a Turn" card, play goes to the other team and no money is awarded. If the player draws the "Bankrupt" card, he or she loses a turn and the team loses all of its money.

★ Players can use their turn to buy a vowel. Price vowels at 200 or 300. Only charge players once for a vowel regardless of how many of that vowel is in the puzzle.

★ Each team guesses one letter at a time and then the next team takes a turn. Keep score on the board.

★ Let team members confer to solve the puzzle. The first team to solve the puzzle wins the round. Play a few rounds. The team with the most money wins the game.

My Aunt Tillie

This game helps identify categories and get kids' brains in gear.

Start off by saying, "My Aunt Tillie went on a trip, and she packed a hat, a coat, and a pair of shoes. Would you like to come?"

Invite a child to reply, "My Aunt Tillie went on a trip, and she packed a hat, a coat, a pair of shoes, and a pair of gloves. May I come?"

Then say, "Yes, you may. Anyone else?" Keep inviting new players to join you. If the children reply correctly they can come along. But those who don't give the correct response must stay home.

The trick is to figure out the category that Aunt Tillie is packing. The categories could be clothes, colors, food, fruit, toys, names, items in alphabetical order, a category in alphabetical order, words that begin with the same letter, progressive numbers—one of one item, two of next, three of next, and so on. There are many categories that you can use.

Memory

Choose one person to begin the game. That person touches an object in the room and then touches another student. The new person touches the same object as the first, then touches another object, and then touches another student. The play continues, with another object added each time, as long as the new student remembers the order of objects.

Quiet

Use this game to quiet down a boisterous class. Choose someone to be "It." Have that person stand in front of the class and look for the quietest classmate. He or she taps the person selected, and they change places. Continue playing until everyone has been tapped and the room is as still as a tomb.

Hide the Object

Hone your students' observation skills with this game. Choose an object in the room (an eraser, ruler, or book) and show it to one row or a group of four or five students. Tell them you are going to hide the object. Have them leave the room. The rest of the class hides the object in plain view.

Have the players return. As soon as a player sees the object he or she sits down, others do the same until all are seated. The first player to sit down hides an object for the next group.

Hide the Object 2

Form two teams. Assign a different item to each team. Hide as many objects as there are players on a team. For example, if there are ten players on a team, hide ten pieces of red candy and ten pieces of white candy. Let the two teams search until they find all the items assigned to their team.

Hide the Object 3 (AKA "Hot & Cold")

Show an object to the class. Ask one person to leave the room while you hide the object. When the player returns, she or he moves around the room. As the player gets closer to the object the others make a loud sound. As the player gets farther away they make a softer sound. Coordinate the sounds with the hidden object: quack for a stuffed duck, make hound dog sounds or cluck for a hidden rubber chicken, or make a ghost sound for a hidden pumpkin.

Play Ball!

While the goal of education is to teach for understanding, students still need to learn key concepts and facts. This often requires memorization, and memorizing can be tedious. Add a little variety to learning multiplication facts or spelling words, and use sports themes to quiz students. In this example the game is baseball. Form two teams. Home plate is the chalkboard. First, second, and third base are desks in their relative positions. You don't have to disrupt your classroom because there's no running.

Have the first player stand at home plate. Ask a question. If the player answers the question correctly he or she goes to first base. If the player doesn't answer the question correctly, she or he is out. Players advance around the bases just like in the real game. Keep score like in a real ballgame, too—three outs and you change sides.

Hoop Dreams

Form two teams. Have the teams stand in rows on opposite sides of the room, facing the chalkboard. Place an empty trash basket in front of the board. Use a soft foam ball or a wad of paper for a ball. Give the first player on Team 1 the ball and ask the player a question. If the player answers correctly, he or she can shoot a basket. Score two points for a correct answer and two points for a basket. Play then moves to the first player on the opposing team. Continue playing until everyone has a chance to answer a question.

Balloon Relay

This game needs to be played in a large space such as an open classroom, a gym, or outdoors. Form two teams. Give each player an inflated balloon. The object of the game is for each player to run from the starting line to the goal (which is a trash basket), deposit the balloon, return to the starting line and tag the next player. All the balloons have to fit into the trash container. (Don't tell students they have to pop them to make them fit!)

Keep 'em Aloft!

This balloon game needs a large open space. Form two teams. Give each team an inflated balloon with a marble in it. The object of the game is to keep the balloon in the air. Make and/or change rules as groups get more proficient, such as: everyone has to touch the balloon at least once before it falls; no one can touch the balloon more than once; or players can use only their heads. Use this game to teach following directions and to incorporate large motor skills and creative physical activity.

Really Funny Relays

These relays have several elements in common. All are played on hands and knees and require a large space to play in.

★ **Lemon Relay.** Form two or more teams. Establish a starting line and finish line. Players take turns rolling a lemon using only a pencil from the starting line to the finish and back again. When the first player finishes, the second player starts. Play continues until the whole team finishes.

* **Paper Cup Relay.** Use the same rules as the game above but move a small paper cup by blowing through a straw.
* **Ping-Pong Ball or Feather Relay.** Use a table tennis ball or a feather. Form two teams. Players attempt to blow the ball or feather into the opposite team's goal. If the ball or feather touches any part of a player's body, the opposing team gets a free turn from center field.

Bite the Dragon's Tail

This game requires a very large space. It's best played in a gym or outside. Have students form a line with three or more players, placing their hands on the waist of the person in front of them. The first person in line is the dragon's head. The last person in line is the tail. The object of the game is for the head to catch the tail by tagging it. The tail tries to avoid being tagged by swinging away without breaking the line. When the tail's been tagged, the person who's the head becomes the tail and the second person in line becomes the new head.

You can also play this with two teams. Each team tries to catch the other team's tail.

Blob Tag

Designate one person as "It." "It" tries to tag someone. The person who gets tagged then holds "Its" hand. Then they try to tag someone else. The line keeps getting bigger and bigger as more people are tagged. Players can't drop hands, and only the two end people can do the tagging.

Caterpillar Race

Form teams of three or more players. Have teams sit on the floor with their legs and arms straddling the person in front of them. Race to the finish line by sliding or bumping along on their bottoms!

Wacky Ball

Play this game in a gym or other large area.

★ Form two teams.

★ Scatter many balls of different sizes and shapes all over the floor—big ones (basketballs, volleyballs), little ones (softballs, tennis balls, Ping-Pong balls), jumbo gym balls, footballs, Nerf balls of different sizes and shapes, balloons, even taped up cardboard boxes.

★ Establish a center line. The object of the game is for one team to get their side clear of balls before they hear the ending signal.

★ Determine the length of play by the age and experience of players. Two minutes is a good starting point.

★ Have players sit on the floor. Explain that they cannot stand up or crawl; they have to move in the sitting position. They can use any part of their body to move the balls, but they can only roll or slide the balls. No throwing is allowed!

★ The team with the least amount of balls on their side at the ending signal wins. Another way of scoring is to assign points to different kinds of balls. The team with the lowest score would be the winner.

More Than Just Fun & Games

By teaching kids recreational skills, movement, and games you introduce them to leisure time activities that help promote health, wellness, and fitness for the rest of their lives. Medical evidence has shown that physical activity is beneficial for cardiovascular health, weight control, longevity, and the reduction of the symptoms of depression and anxiety. If humor and health aren't enough, these games and exercises also help to strengthen gross and fine motor skills, spatial awareness, and coordination. So, move around a little, giggle, get healthy, and learn.

Wheel of Fortune Cards

Game Props for Teachers & Students

Photocopy and cut apart the cards. Use them to play the game described on page 167.

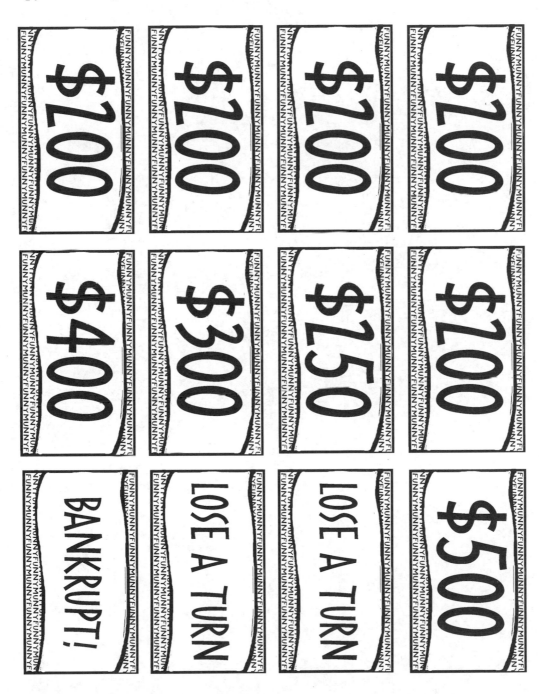

A Not-So-Final word

The whole object of comedy is to be yourself and the closer you get to that, the funnier you will be."
—JERRY SEINFELD

I haven't told any jokes throughout this whole book, but I'd like to leave you with one.

One morning a mother hurried to her son's bedroom door and knocked loudly. "Morris! Morris!" she yelled. "Get up! You're going to be late for school!"

"But, Mom," Morris whined, "I don't wanna go to school."

"You have to, Morris," his mother said, throwing open the bedroom door. "Get up. Get dressed. Wash behind your ears. Eat your breakfast. And go to school."
"But, Mom, I don't wanna go to school," Morris kept whining.

"What's gotten into you, Morris?" his mother asked. "All of a sudden you don't want to go to school."

"I hate school," said Morris. "The teachers don't like me. The kids call me names and throw things at me."

"Morris, Morris," pleaded his mother, *you–have–to–go–to–school!*"

"But why, Mom?" Morris cried.

"For two reasons," said his mother. "First, you're forty-five years old, and second, you're the principal."

Okay, if we "havta" be here, at least it can be fun.

I hope that as you've read this book, you've tried out many of the ideas. If they were successful, congratulations! If they weren't, congratulations anyway—at least you tried. I bet you got some kind of laugh, or a grin or a chuckle. I accept even a groan as a laugh on some of my corny stuff.

Now that you've gotten your feet wet, I hope you go back and reread the book and try out some ideas you were too timid to try the first time around. Work on getting just one or two smiles a day. Carry your humor journal around with you. Take it out and look at it when you're having a bad day. Keep adding to it when you're having a good day. Find some new "random acts of craziness" to perform.

Remember, novelty in the classroom is a good thing. It gives the brain something to work on. It excites the learning processes. Humor is a valuable educational tool, and one worth cultivating. You have to both work at and play with humor. When you see or hear a funny idea, write it down. But don't let it just sit in your little black book. Think about it, give it life, put it to work, and use it with your students.

I'd love to hear about some of your ideas. If you've tried some of the suggestions in this book, revised others, and thought of some new ones, let me know. With your ideas and a ton of others I still have, we could probably write *Laughing Lessons, the Second Semester.*

Keep smiling!

Really Fun Resources

Fun Books for Early Elementary Children

Alberg, Janet, and Allan Alberg. *The Jolly Postman* (Boston: Little, Brown & Co., 1986). A Jolly Postman delivers letters to several famous fairy tale characters such as the Big Bad Wolf, Cinderella, and the Three Bears.

Barrett, Judi. *Cloudy with a Chance of Meatballs* (New York: Aladdin Books, 1982). Life is delicious in the town of Chewandswallow, where it rains soup and juice, snows mashed potatoes, and blows storms of hamburgers—until the weather takes a turn for the worse.

Barrett, Judi. *Pickles to Pittsburgh* (New York: Atheneum, 1997). In this sequel to *Cloudy with a Chance of Meatballs,* the characters find themselves back in the town of Chewandswallow.

Baylor, Byrd. *Everybody Needs a Rock* (New York: Aladdin Books, 1987). Describes the qualities to consider in selecting the perfect rock for play and pleasure.

Brown, Marc. *Arthur Babysits* (Boston: Little, Brown & Co., 1994). Arthur's experience baby-sitting for the terrible Tibble twins is as challenging as he expected, but he finally gets control by telling them a spooky story.

Charlip, Remy. *Fortunately* (New York: Aladdin Books, 1993). Good luck and bad luck accompany Ned from New York to Florida on his way to a surprise party.

Cooney, Barbara. *Miss Rumphius* (New York: Viking, 1985). Seeking adventure in faraway places, Miss Rumphius fulfills her dream of living by the sea in her old age, and then sets out to make the world more beautiful.

Fox, Mem. *Night Noises* (San Diego: Harcourt Brace, 1992). Old Lily Laceby dozes by the fire with her faithful dog at her feet as strange night noises herald a surprising awakening.

Fox, Mem. *Shoes from Grandpa* (New York: Orchard Books, 1992). In a cumulative rhyme, family members describe the clothes they intend to give Jessie to go with her shoes from Grandpa.

Munsch, Robert. *50 Below Zero* (Toronto: Annick, 1989). Jason's dad walks in his sleep, and Jason finds him in the most unlikely places.

Munsch, Robert. *I Have To Go!* (Buffalo, NY: Firefly Books, 1989). Despite all the anxious preparations and inquiries of his parents, little Andrew maintains his own individual sense of timing and appropriateness.

Munsch, Robert. *Love You Forever* (Buffalo, NY: Firefly Books, 1995). This is a gentle affirmation of the love parents feel for their child—forever.

Munsch, Robert. *The Paper Bag Princess* (Toronto: Annick, 1995). A beautiful princess comes to the rescue of her less-than-thankful prince, who has been kidnapped by a dragon.

Munsch, Robert. *Show and Tell* (Toronto: Annick, 1991). Ben wanted to take something really neat to school for show and tell, so he decided to take his new baby sister.

Munsch, Robert. *Wait and See* (Toronto: Annick, 1993). Olivia confidently warns her parents that her birthday wish will come true, and when snow does begin to fall in the middle of summer, piling up against the door, her parents rush to whip up another cake so she can wish for a "solution."

Numeroff, Laura Joffe. *If You Give a Mouse a Cookie* (New York: HarperCollins, 1985). A boy offers a passing mouse a cookie, prompting the need for a glass of milk, then a straw, and so on in this story about an energetic mouse and an accommodating little boy.

Parrish, Peggy. *Amelia Bedelia* (New York: HarperFestival, 1999). A literal-minded housekeeper causes a ruckus in the household when she attempts to make sense of some instructions.

Pilkey, Dav. *Dog Breath* (New York: Scholastic, 1994). Although Hally Tosis is a good dog, her owners want to find a new home for her, because she has perfectly horrible breath, until Hally's breath saves the day.

Pilkey, Dav. *Dogzilla* (San Diego: Harcourt Brace, 1993). When Dogzilla invades Mousopolis, the rodent inhabitants must decide on a plan to rid themselves of this terrible menace before their city is chewed to pieces.

Pilkey, Dav. *The Hallo-Wiener* (New York: Scholastic, 1999). Humiliated by his hot-dog Halloween costume, Oscar the dachshund endures ridicule from his canine friends and eventually proves that while he's short on height, he's long on heart.

Pilkey, Dav. *Kat Kong* (San Diego: Harcourt Brace, 1993). This spoof of the story of King Kong takes place in Mousopolis with mice and cat characters.

Pilkey, Dav, and Sue Denim. *The Dumb Bunnies* (New York: Scholastic, 1998). In this parody of a fairy tale, Little Red Goldilocks makes herself at home in the Bunny house while Momma, Poppa, and Baby Bunny enjoy a day out on the town.

Pinkwater, Daniel Manus. *Fat Men From Space* (New York: Yearling Books, 1980). While William is held captive in a spaceship, alien armies land and wipe out the earth's supply of junk foods. He escapes, but humans must learn to like the foods left behind: wholegrain bread, milk, vegetables, all the healthy foods.

Pinkwater, Daniel Manus. *Hoboken Chicken Emergency* (New York: Aladdin Books, 1999). Arthur is sent out to bring home the family's Thanksgiving turkey, but instead he returns with Henrietta—a 266-pound chicken with a mind of her own.

Sacher, Louis. *Marvin Redpost: Kidnapped at Birth?* (New York: Random House, 1992). Certain that he is not Marvin Redpost but Robert, the lost Prince of Shampoo, Marvin prepares to break the news to the parents who, he is sure, adopted him years ago.

Sendak, Maurice. *Chicken Soup with Rice* (New York: Harper Trophy, 1991). Poems and illustrations help to teach young children the months of the year.

Dr. Seuss. *The Foot Book* (New York: Random House, 1996). A classic Seuss book, which teaches young children the concept of opposites.

Waber, Bernard. *Ira Sleeps Over* (Boston: Houghton Mifflin, 1979). Ira is thrilled to spend the night at Reggie's until his sister raises the question of whether or not he should take his teddy bear.

Wiseman, Bernard. *Morris and Boris at the Circus* (New York: Harper Trophy, 1990). Morris and Boris go to the circus as spectators and end up being part of the action.

Chapter Books & Other Fun Things for Older Elementary Kids

Adler, David A. *Cam Jansen and the Mystery of the Dinosaur Bones* (New York: Puffin Books, 1997). When she notices some bones missing from a dinosaur skeleton exhibited in the museum, a young girl with a photographic memory tries to discover who has been taking them and why.

Babbitt, Natalie. *Tuck Everlasting* (New York: Farrar, Straus & Giroux, 1986). Ten-year-old Winnie discovers the magic spring that has given the Tuck family eternal life and faces the difficult decision of whether or not to drink from it.

Baum, L. Frank. *The Wizard of Oz* (New York: Henry Holt & Co., 1988). A tornado sends a young girl to the land of Oz where she must travel down a yellow brick road to the Wizard, who, she is told, can help her get back home to Kansas. Along the way she meets the Scarecrow, Tin Woodsman, Cowardly Lion, and the Wicked Witch of the West.

Cleary, Beverly. *The Mouse and the Motorcycle* (New York: Avon Books, 1990). A reckless young mouse named Ralph meets a boy who teaches Ralph how to ride his toy motorcycle, and the adventure begins.

Cleary, Beverly. *Ralph S. Mouse* (New York: Avon Books, 1993). The adventures of a motorcycle-riding mouse who goes to school and becomes the instigator of an investigation of rodents and the peacemaker for two lonely boys.

Cleary, Beverly. *Ramona's World* (New York: Morrow Junior Books, 1999). Ramona Quimby is now in the fourth grade. She has to compete for attention with a new baby sister and her perfect older sister.

Cleary, Beverly. *Ramona the Pest* (New York: Avon Books, 1996). The tale of young Ramona Quimby's first days in kindergarten and the trials and delights of beginning school.

Cleary, Beverly. *Runaway Ralph* (New York: Avon Books, 1991). Ralph, the mouse, runs away from home looking for freedom from his bossy mother and pesky siblings and ends up having the adventure of a lifetime.

Clements, Andrew. *Double Trouble in Walla Walla* (Brookfield, CT: Millbrook Press, 1997). It's an ordinary morning in Walla Walla until Lulu, her teacher, the school nurse, and the principal are all infected by a word warp which makes them reduplicate everything they say.

Clements, Andrew. *Frindle* (New York: Aladdin Books, 1998). When Nick decides to turn his fifth grade teacher's love of the dictionary around on her, he invents a new word and begins a chain of events that quickly moves beyond his control.

Eager, Edward. *Half Magic* (San Diego: Harcourt Brace, 1999). Four children discover a "half magic" coin and their following adventures mix magic and reality. *Knight's Castle, The Time Garden,* and *Magic by the Lake* are sequels to this popular tale.

Howe, Deborah, and James Howe. *Bunnicula* (New York: Aladdin Books, 1996). When the Monroe family brings home a bunny they found in a movie theater while watching *Dracula,* Chester the cat and Harold the dog are suspicious of the new resident. When all the vegetables suddenly turn white, they believe him to be a vegetarian vampire.

Juster, Norton. *The Phantom Tollbooth* (New York: Random House, 1993). Discovering a large toy tollbooth in his room, bored ten-year-old Milo drives through the tollbooth's gates and begins a memorable journey to the Kingdom of Wisdom with a watchdog named Tuck.

Konigsburg, E.L. *From the Mixed-Up Files of Mrs. Basil E. Frankweiler* (New York: Aladdin Books, 1967). Having run away with her younger brother to live in the Metropolitan Museum of Art, twelve-year-old Claudia strives to keep things in order in their new home and to become a changed person and a heroine to herself.

Lindgren, Astrid. *Pippi Longstocking* (New York: Puffin Books, 1997). Escapades of a lucky little girl who lives with a horse and a monkey—but without any parents—at the edge of a Swedish village.

Pilkey, Dav. *The Adventures of Captain Underpants* (New York: Little Apple, 1997). George and Harold create a comic book superhero, Captain Underpants, and hypnotize their school principal into assuming his identity.

Pinkwater, Daniel Manus. *5 Novels* (New York: Farrar, Straus & Giroux, 1997). This collection of Pinkwater's novels includes *Alan Mendelsohn, the Boy from Mars; Slaves of Spiegel; The Snarkout Boys and the Avocado of Death; The Last Guru;* and *Young Adult Novel.*

Pinkwater, Daniel Manus. *Lizard Music* (New York: Bantam Books, 1996). When left to take care of himself, a young boy becomes involved with a community of intelligent lizards who tell him of a little-known invasion from outer space.

Pinkwater, Daniel Manus. *The Magic Goose* (New York: Apple, 1997). This is the adventure of a goose who goes in search of magic.

Rowling, J.K. *Harry Potter and the Sorcerer's Stone* (New York: Arthur A. Levine Books, 1998). Rescued from the outrageous neglect of his aunt and uncle, a young boy with a great destiny proves his worth while attending Hogwarts School for Wizards and Witches. *Harry Potter and the Chamber of Secrets* and *Harry Potter and the Prisoner of Azkaban* are also part of this series.

Sachar, Louis. *Sideways Stories from Wayside School* (New York: Avon Books, 1993). Humorous episodes from the classroom on the thirtieth floor of Wayside School, which was accidentally built sideways with one classroom on each story.

Sachar, Louis. *There's a Boy in the Girls' Bathroom* (New York: Random House, 1994). An unmanageable, but lovable, eleven-year-old misfit learns to believe in himself when he gets to know the new school counselor, who is a sort of misfit, too.

White, E.B. *Charlotte's Web* (New York: Harper Trophy, 1999). Wilbur, a lovable pig, is rescued from a cruel fate by a beautiful and intelligent spider named Charlotte.

White, E.B. *Stuart Little* (New York: HarperCollins, 1974). The adventures of the debonair mouse Stuart Little as he sets out in the world to seek out his dearest friend, a little bird who stayed a few days in his family's garden.

Cartooning & Comics

Blitz, Bruce. *Blitz the Big Book of Cartooning* (Philadelphia: Courage Books, 1998). This is a fun, comprehensive, and easy-to-use guide to cartoon drawing.

Gagline: The Unique Cartoon Caption Game (Invisions, Inc., 815 Bundy Drive, Los Angeles, CA 90049). A game for coming up with captions for cartoons.

Greenberg, Dan. *Comic-Strip Math* (New York: Scholastic, 1999). Cartoons and funny story problems help to build math skills.

Hart, Christopher. *Drawing on the Funny Side of the Brain: How to Come Up with Jokes for Cartoons and Comic Strips* (New York: Watson-Guptill, 1998). This book not only explains how to draw funny cartoons and characters, but most importantly, it tells how to come up with funny ideas.

Heath, Mark. *Drawing Cartoons (First Steps Series)* (Cincinnati, OH: North Light Books, 1998). Breaks down cartooning into easy step-by-step drawings.

Moberg, Randy. *TNT Teaching: Over 200 Dynamite Ways to Make Your Classroom Come Alive* (Minneapolis: Free Spirit Publishing, 1994). This book not only offers funny ideas to spice up your teaching, it also offers basic techniques for beginners in cartooning.

Creativity

Barrett, Susan L. *It's All In Your Head: A Guide to Understanding Your Brain and Boosting Your Brain Power* (Minneapolis: Free Spirit Publishing, 1992). Tells about the mysteries of the brain and offers ideas on how to be more creative.

Freed, Jeffery. *Right-Brained Children in a Left-Brained World* (New York: Simon & Schuster, 1997). This book offers a step-by-step program that shows parents how to work with, not against, the special abilities of the attention deficit disorder (ADD) child.

Perry, Susan K. *Playing Smart* (Minneapolis: Free Spirit Publishing, 2001). Some wonderful, funny, and offbeat activities for working with kids.

Roukes, Nicholas. *Humor in Art: A Celebration of Visual Wit* (Worchester, MA: Davis Publications, 1997). Discover visual humor and see the funny side of art in this book divided into six chapters: wit, whimsy, parody, satire, comic nonsense, and surrealism.

Discipline

Beane, Allan L., Ph.D. *The Bully Free Classroom* (Minneapolis: Free Spirit Publishing, 1999). Ideas to help you create a positive classroom environment using prevention and intervention strategies.

MacKenzie, Robert J. *Setting Limits in the Classroom* (Rocklin, CA: Prima Publishing, 1996). Offers sound advice for teachers on topics such as creating individual structures that work, stopping power struggles before they start, and using supportive words with effective action.

Nelsen, Jane. *Positive Discipline in the Classroom* (Rocklin, CA: Prima Publishing, 1997). Three parenting experts address the concept of class meetings, where students and teachers work together to solve problems.

Humor & You

Allen, Steve. *How To Be Funny* (Amherst, NY: Prometheus Books, 1998). This book will help you to discover the comic in you and show you how to be funny in your personal life.

Allen, Steve. *Make 'Em Laugh* (Amherst, NY: Prometheus Books, 1993). This book will help you to develop your own unique talent for being funny.

Carter, Judy. *Stand-Up Comedy* (New York: Dell Books, 1989). Offers a lot of good advice on being an effective communicator and having a happier, funnier life.

McGhee, Paul E., Ph.D. *How to Develop Your Sense of Humor* (Dubuque, IA: Kendall/Hunt Publishing, 1994). Dr. McGhee shows how to analyze and develop your sense of humor. The book is currently out of print, but worth finding at the library.

Humor in the Classroom

Hill, Deborah J., Ph.D. *Humor in the Classroom* (Springfield, IL: Charles C. Thomas, 1988). A handbook for teachers on humor and telling jokes in the classroom. This book uses a very didactic approach in presenting the material. It explains every joke and nuance in minute detail, such as what is a malaprop? What is a comeback? What is an oxymoron?

Loomans, Diane, and Karen Kolberg. *The Laughing Classroom* (Tiburon, CA: H.J. Kramer, 1993). Offers many old and new ideas for play breaks to teach with humor.

Shade, Richard A. *License to Laugh* (Englewood, CO: Teacher Ideas Press, 1996). Explains the different types of humor and gives small examples on how to apply this humor to the classroom.

Humor Research with Children

Fry, William F. *Sweet Madness: A Study of Humor* (Palo Alto, CA: Pacific Books, 1970). This book is out of print, but should be available at your local public library.

Kohn, Alfie. *The Schools Our Children Deserve* (New York: Houghton Mifflin, 1999). The author critiques traditional public schooling and the "Old School" where teachers rely on lectures, textbooks, worksheets, and grades.

McGhee, Paul E., Ph.D. *Children's Humour* (New York: John Wiley & Sons, 1980). This book is out of print, but should be available at your local public library.

McGhee, Paul E., Ph.D. *Humor and Children's Development: A Guide to Practical Applications* (Binghamton, NY: Haworth Press, 1989). Geared toward practical applications of humor with children this instructive volume illustrates how to effectively incorporate humor into children's lives to produce enormously positive results.

McGhee, Paul E., Ph.D., and Jefferey H. Goldstein. *Handbook of Humor Research, Vols. 1 & 2* (New York: Springer-Verlag, 1983). These books are out of print, but should be available at your local public library.

Pert, Candace B. *Molecules of Emotion: Why You Feel the Way You Feel* (New York: Scribner, 1997). The author explains the groundbreaking experiments that prove that the mind and the body are not two separate entities, but are one interconnected information system—the mindbody.

Weaver, Richard L., and Howard W. Cotrell. "Ten Specific Techniques for Developing Humor in the Classroom." *Educational Journal.* Vol. 108, no. 2, pp. 167–179.

Jokes

Burgess, Ron. *Clown Jokes & Walkaround Gags* (Colorado Springs, CO: Piccadilly Books, 1998). This book is loaded with jokes and clown cartoons—good clean fun for all ages.

Burgess, Ron. *Son of Clown Jokes & Walkaround Gags* (Colorado Springs, CO: Piccadilly Books, 2000). This is the sequel to *Clown Jokes & Walkaround Gags* with more zany clown jokes, cartoons, and sight gags.

Rosenbloom, Joseph. *Gigantic Joke Book* (New York: Sterling Publishing Co., 1989). This book presents more than 1,000 jokes on wide-ranging topics.

Rosenbloom, Joseph, and Mike Artell. *The Little Giant Book of Tongue Twisters* (New York: Sterling Publishing Co., 1999). This book contains hundreds of wacky word combinations.

Juggling

Cassidy, John, et al. *Juggling for the Complete Klutz* (Palo Alto, CA: Klutz Inc, 1994). Like all of the Klutz books, this is a complete basic course. It also comes with juggling bean bags.

Irving, Robert, and Mike Martins. *Pathways in Juggling: Learn How to Juggle with Balls, Clubs, Devil Sticks, Diabolos, and Beyond* (Buffalo, NY: Firefly Books, 1997). Color photographs and diagrams, accompanied by tips and reminders, make this a great book for beginners learning how to juggle.

Woodburn, Bob. *The Instant Juggling Book with 3 Juggling Balls* (Buffalo, NY: Firefly Books, 1990). This book comes with three soft, weighty juggling balls to get you started right away.

Magic

Bauer, Caroline Feller. *Leading Kids to Books Through Magic* (Chicago: American Library Association, 1996). This book shows how to use magic tricks to entertain children and lead them to good books and how to bolster their courage and use magic to promote reading.

Eldin, Peter. *The Magic Handbook* (New York: Aladdin Books, 1985). If you only buy one magic book, buy this little gem. It explains magic with money, ropes, cards, and other paraphernalia.

Evans, Cheryl, et al. *The Usborne Complete Book of Magic* (Tulsa, OK: EDC Publishing, 1991). Magic tricks easily explained.

Ogden, Tom. *The Complete Idiot's Guide to Magic Tricks* (New York: Alpha Books, 1999). A quick, easy, fool-proof way to learn some very good basic tricks. It even has some arithmetic tricks.

Math, Science, & Social Studies

Allison, Linda, and David Katz. *Gee, Wiz! How to Mix Art and Science, or the Art of Thinking Scientifically* (Boston: Little, Brown & Co., 1983). The authors use art to explore science with fun experiments to challenge the imagination.

Branzei, Sylvia. *Grossology* (New York: Penguin, 1996). All the gross, disgusting things that come from our bodies are explained in detail. Kids love all of this stomach-turning stuff. Also in the series are: *Grossology Begins at Home, Virtual Grossology, Animal Grossology,* and *Hands-On Grossology.*

Kenda, Margaret, and Phyllis S. Williams. *Geography Wizardry for Kids* (Hauppauge, NY: Barron's Educational Series, Inc., 1997). Over 150 fun projects, maps, games, crafts, and experiments for junior explorers. Includes a glossary of terms and map symbols.

Kenda, Margaret, and Phyllis S. Williams. *Math Wizardry for Kids* (Hauppauge, NY: Barron's Educational Series, Inc., 1995). Over 200 fun and challenging math puzzles, games, designs, and projects. Includes a glossary of terms, math signs, and symbols.

Kenda, Margaret, and Phyllis S. Williams. *Science Wizardry for Kids* (Hauppauge, NY: Barron's Educational Series, Inc., 1992). More than 200 experiments that use inexpensive items and materials available in every household. Includes a glossary of terms.

Kohl, Mary Ann, and Jean Potter. *Science Arts* (Bellingham, WA: Bright Ring, 1993). This book builds on children's natural curiosity to discover science concepts through art experiments.

Maganzini, Christy. *Cool Math: Math Tricks, Amazing Math Activities, Cool Calculations, Awesome Math Factoids, and More* (New York: Price Stern Sloan, 1997). Packed with codes, games, quizzes, hands-on activities, and mind-bending facts, this book proves, beyond a doubt, that math is anything but boring.

Mitumasa, Anno. *Anno's Math Games* (New York: Paper Star, 1997). Lively pictures and intriguing puzzles and games take young children on a fun-filled journey through basic mathematical concepts, showing how math skills are used every day.

Sabbeth, Alex. *Rubber-Band Banjos and a Java Jive Bass* (New York: John Wiley & Sons, 1997). A noisy trip through the important instruments, people, and compositions of sound and music demonstrates the way musical sound is made and heard while inviting readers to make and play on homemade instruments.

Schwartz, David, and Steven Kellogg. *How Much Is a Million?* (New York: Mulberry Books, 1993). Children are often intrigued by or confused about very large numbers. Simple concepts help readers conceptualize astronomical numbers like a million, billion, and trillion.

VanCleave, Janice. *200 Gooey, Slippery, Slimy, Weird & Fun Experiments* (New York: John Wiley & Sons, 1992). Two hundred easy-to-do experiments that are safe and fun.

VanCleave, Janice. *201 Awesome, Magical, Bizarre, & Incredible Experiments* (New York: John Wiley & Sons, 1994). A sequel to her first book, with even more fun science experiments.

VanCleave, Janice. *203 Icy, Freezing, Frosty, Cool & Wild Experiments* (New York: John Wiley & Sons, 1999). VanCleave's latest volume in her creative and fun science experiment series.

Wood, Robert W. *Sound FUNdamentals: Funtastic Science Activities for Kids* (Philadelphia: Chelsea House Publishers, 1999). This has many fresh experiments to captivate youngsters and build their interest in science. A total of 37 experiments demystify the phenomena of acoustics and hearing. Activities are quick and simple and can be completed using simple household materials.

Music

Best of Schoolhouse Rock. Various artists (Atlantic, 1998). Available on CD or cassette, this compilation includes some of the witty educational songs that appeared during Saturday morning cartoons in the 1970s and 1980s. Also available are *Grammar Rock, Multiplication Rock, America Rock,* and *Science Rock*.

Krull, Kathleen. *Gonna Sing My Head Off! American Folk Songs for Children* (New York: Knopf, 1995). This anthology includes complete lyrics, arrangements, and historical notes for songs from over two centuries of American musical history.

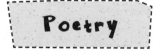

Poetry

Lansky, Bruce. *Kids Pick the Funniest Poems* (Minneapolis: Meadowbrook Press, 1991). A collection of humorous poems selected by a panel of children, featuring an all-star cast of poets from Dr. Seuss and Shel Silverstein to Judith Viorst and Jack Prelutsky.

Prelutsky, Jack. *For Laughing Out Loud* (New York: Knopf, 1991). A collection of humorous poems by writers including Ellen Raskin, Karla Kuskin, Ogden Nash, and Arnold Lobel.

Prelutsky, Jack. *The New Kid on the Block* (New York: Greenwillow Books, 1984). Humorous poems about such strange creatures and people as Baloney Belly Billy and the Gloopy Gloopers.

Rosen, Michael. *Walking the Bridge of Your Nose* (New York: Larousse Kingfisher Chambers, 1999). Full-color artwork complements a zany collection of wordplay in verse, including poetry, rhymes, riddles, tongue twisters, limericks, and more.

Silverstein, Shel. *Falling Up* (New York: HarperCollins, 1996). A collection of more than one hundred poems and drawings that introduce characters such as Allison Beals and her 25 Eels, Danny O'Dare the Dancin' Bear, Headphone Harry, and many others.

Silverstein, Shel. *A Light in the Attic* (New York: HarperCollins, 1981). A collection of humorous poems and drawings.

Silverstein, Shel. *Where the Sidewalk Ends* (New York: HarperCollins, 1974). A boy who turns into a TV set and a girl who eats a whale are only two of the characters in a collection of humorous poetry illustrated with the author's own drawings.

Viorst, Judith. *If I Were in Charge of the World & Other Worries* (New York: Aladdin Books, 1984). If you've ever had trouble apologizing or keeping a secret, had a crush or a broken heart, here are forty-one poems that reveal a variety of secret thoughts, worries, and wishes written with humor and understanding.

Puppets

Bauer, Caroline Feller. *Leading Kids to Books Through Puppets* (Chicago: American Library Association, 1997). This book has really easy puppets to make and use, plus great puppet scripts.

Hanford, Robert Ten Eyck. *The Complete Book of Puppets and Puppeteering* (New York: Drake, 1976). Everything on puppets, from buying and designing to scripts, props, stages, and lighting. It is a complete puppet course. Although this book is out of print, you should be able to find it at your local public library.

Henson, Cheryl. *The Muppets Make Puppets!* (New York: Workman Publishing, 1994). How to create, make, and use puppets from the junk you have around. The book even comes with its own junk—feathers, eyes, and other things.

Storytelling

Bauer, Caroline Feller. *New Handbook for Storytellers* (Chicago: American Library Association, 1993). Everything you could possibly want to know about storytelling and running a storytelling program is in this book, from equipment and promotions to poems and stories to tell.

Bauer, Caroline Feller. *Read For the Fun of It* (Bronx, NY: H.W. Wilson Co., 1992). Storytelling using puppets, magic, and other visual aids.

Bay, Jeanette Graham. *A Treasury of Flannel-Board Stories* (Fort Atkinson, WI: Highsmith Press LLC, 1995). Twenty stories created for the flannelboard. Includes scripts and patterns.

Irving, Jan, and Robin Currie. *Raising the Roof* (Englewood, CO: Teacher Idea Press, 1991). Children's stories and activities using the house as a theme. Eight separate themes with ideas, poems, read-aloud stories, draw-and-tell stories, and puppets.

Mallett, Jerry, and Timothy Ervin. *Fold and Cut Stories* (Fort Atkinson, WI: Highsmith Press LLC, 1993). Sixteen cut-and-fold stories that create mystery answers for each.

Mallett, Jerry, and Timothy Ervin. *Sound and Action Stories* (Fort Atkinson, WI: Highsmith Press LLC, 1993). Twenty stories for children to listen to and respond to with claps, animal noises, and actions.

Marsh, Valerie. *Paper Cutting Stories From A to Z* (Fort Atkinson, WI: Highsmith Press LLC, 1992). A story to tell about each letter of the alphabet while you cut shapes from paper. Each of the 26 stories is a riddle and the answer is the cutout.

Thompson, Richard. *Frog's Riddle & Other Draw and Tell Stories* (Toronto: Annick, 1990). Step-by-step instructions on how to do 12 draw-and-tell stories.

Catalogs

Archie McPhee & Company
P.O. Box 30852
Seattle, WA 98113
(425) 349-3009
www.mcphee.com
The *Archie McPhee* catalog has tons of gag items, and you'll have to be selective. Some items may be offensive, but you'll find a wealth of ideas here.

Bits & Pieces
1 Puzzle Place, B8016
Stevens Point, WI 54481
1-800-JIGSAWS (1-800-544-7297)
www.bitsandpieces.com
A puzzle catalog that includes hundreds of puzzles, jigsaws, crosswords, three dimensionals, word puzzles, illusions, and mind challenges.

Hank Lee's Magic Factory
P.O. Box 789
Medford, MA 02155
1-800-874-7400
www.magicfact.com
There are a lot of magic dealers but I think Hank Lee's has the fastest delivery of all of them. His huge catalog is tremendous.

HomeRoom
P.O. Box 388
Centerbrook, CT 06409
1-800-222-8270
www.homeroomcatalog.com
HomeRoom catalog has great gifts that other people should buy you, but if that doesn't happen you can buy them for yourself. Terrific shirts, sweaters, and room decorations.

Into The Wind
1408 Pearl Street
Boulder, CO 80302
1-800-541-0314
www.intothewind.com
When someone tells you to go fly a kite, this is the catalog to help you. There are terrific kites and other great flying and throwing apparatus. Many are perfect for science experiments.

Jeannie's Kids Club
7835 Freedom Avenue NW
North Canton, OH 44720
1-800-363-0500
www.kidsstuff.com
This online catalog features imaginative and interactive products that keep kids engaged and interested in learning.

The Lighter Side
P.O. Box 25600
Bradenton, FL 34206
1-800-668-6174
www.lighterside.com
Lighthearted gifts, delightful surprises, decorations, T-shirts, and much more. Great stuff to fill up your classroom with laughter.

Music K–8 Marketplace
Plank Road Publishing, Inc.
P.O. Box 26627
Wauwatosa, WI 53226
1-800-437-0832
www.musick8.com
This 45-page catalog lists collections of children's songs, ethnic songs, classical, rock, and rap. It also has videos and recordings of music by many different instruments from around the world—Africa, India, East Asia, Ireland, South America, Middle East, and Native American. It also offers books of creative, imaginative ways to present musical performances, use musical games, and make music in unusual ways.

Oriental Trading Company
P.O. Box 3407
Omaha, NE 68103
1-800-875-8480
www.oriental.com
I think every teacher in the world has heard about this company. If you haven't, you're in for a surprise. They have more doo-dads and thing-a-ma-jigs than you can count, from pencils and room decorations to key chains and grab-bag gifts.

Rhode Island Novelty
19 Industrial Lane
Johnston, RI 02919
1-800-528-5599
www.rinovelty.com
R.I. Novelty has as many, or more, of the same items as *Oriental Trading:* novelties, small giftware, small give-away toys, costumes, jokes, jewelry, and tons of other things.

SmileMakers
P.O. Box 2543
Spartanburg, SC 29304
1-800-825-8085
www.smilemakers.com
Loaded with fun stuff for the classroom, plus more stickers than you could ever possibly need. They have stickers for everything—Barbie, Mr. Potato Head, The Berenstain Bears, The Rugrats, Clifford the Big Red Dog, Curious George, Babe—you name it, they have a sticker.

Spilsbury Puzzle Co.
3650 Milwaukee Street
P.O. Box 8922
Madison, WI 53708
1-800-285-8619
www.spilsbury.com
Loaded with puzzles, games, and gifts for all ages and at all prices.

Tannen's Magic
Louis Tannen, Inc.
24 W. 25th Street, 2nd Floor
New York, NY 10010
(212) 929-4500
www.tannens.com
Another magic dealer with a large catalog.

Things You Never Knew Existed
Johnson Smith Company
P.O. Box 25600
Bradenton, FL 34206
1-800-843-0762
www.johnsonsmith.com
The ultimate catalog. It delivers what the title says plus even more. Many of the props and tricks that I've mentioned, like the microphone, phony telephone, fly swatters, to name just a few, are in this catalog, plus hundreds more. There are things like a backward clock, hats for every occasion or activity, signs, T-shirts, and other fun items just too numerous to mention.

Extra Added Attractions

Clowns of America International
P.O. Box Clown
Richeyville, PA 15358
1-888-52-CLOWN (1-888-522-5696)
www.coai.org
Organization of amateur and professional clowns. Their journal is *The New Calliope*. It offers quite a bit of information on clowns and clowning.

The Humor Project, Inc.
480 Broadway, Suite 210
Saratoga Springs, NY 12866
(518) 587-8770
www.HumorProject.com
Quarterly journal is called *Laughing Matters*. They have a great catalog of humor books & videos (for teachers, trainers, speakers, and business people).

International Brotherhood of Magicians

11155 South Towne Square, Suite C
St. Louis, MO 63123
(314) 845-9200
www.magician.org
One of the many fine magician's societies. Their journal is called *The Linking Ring.*

International Jugglers Association

P.O. Box 112550
Carrollton, TX 75011
(415) 596-3307
www.juggle.org
Society of juggling friends with 3000 members. Has a bimonthly publication—*Juggle* magazine.

Puppeteers of America

P.O. Box 29417
Parma, OH 44129
1-888-568-6235
www.puppeteers.org
A very good organization for anyone interested in puppets. They have a newsletter, a quarterly journal *(Puppetry Journal),* and a puppetry store. Very interesting and informative group.

Society of American Magicians

P.O. Box 510260
St. Louis, MO 63151
www.magicsam.com
You could join an organization that Harry Houdini belonged to and was a past president of. Their journal is called *M-U-M.*

World Clown Association

P.O. Box 77236
Corona, CA 92877
1-800-336-7922
www.worldclownassociation.com
Organization of amateur and professional clowns. Their journal, *Clowning Around,* is published eight times a year.

Internet and Other Computer-Related Stuff

The Internet is loaded with information on puppets, magic, juggling, teacher stuff, teacher humor, plus, as you probably already know, a zillion other things. Just log onto your favorite search engine, type the keyword, and like magic you have a reference library in your home.

Card Trick Central
web.superb.net/cardtric/
This site delivers hundreds of card tricks with instructions and, in some cases, illustrations. Kids can also submit their own tricks to the site.

Clown Jokes & Gags from Ron Burgess
www.members.tripod.com/~sillywillytheclown
This is my Web site. It has kid jokes, nursery rhyme jokes, and clown jokes. The first three links are to my other Web sites. They have links to Web sites of magic, juggling, puppets, yo-yos, Mr. Potato Head, and teacher humor.

Discovery's School Puzzlemaker
puzzlemaker.school.discovery.com
This page is part of an awesome Web site hosted by the Discovery Channel *(www.school.discovery.com)*. You can create your own mazes, word puzzles, crosswords, and more! Click on the site's homepage to access all sorts of other great learning activities, like exciting science projects, games, and other fun stuff.

The Family Poet
www.familypoet.com
This Web page contains a hilarious collection of poetry for all ages. Some of the poems are illustrated.

Free Graphics
www.freegraphics.com
This site links to several other sites that offer free graphics and animation. Each site is ranked based on the quality and quantity of its graphics.

FunBrain.com
FunBrain.com
This site contains loads of games, quizzes, and fun activities for kids of all ages. It boasts being "The Internet's #1 site for K–8 teachers and kids."

Kid Pix Studio Deluxe (Broderbund Software, Inc.)
This software for ages 3–12 gives kids six unique painting, drawing, and animation projects to select from. You can create your own cartoons!

KidsArt

www.kidsart.com

This site offers art activities for kids, some of which can be downloaded for free. An online catalog includes teaching materials, games, and learning enrichment activities.

KinderArt

www.kinderart.com

This site provides free art lesson plans, reference material, and an online kid's gallery. There are activities for all ages, and they are divided into seasonal, multicultural, recycling, sculpture, cross curriculum, and many more categories.

Story Palace

storypalace.ourfamily.com/main2.html

This site is the place to read, to learn, and to share wisdom at the same time. It provides three main sections: Inspirational Stories, Jokes & Humor, and Children's Stories.

The Yuckiest Site on the Internet

yucky.kids.discovery.com

Find quizzes, trivia, interesting facts, games, links to more yucky sites, and more at the Yuckiest Site. It has a section for parents and teachers, too.

Index

Locators in **bold** indicate reproducible pages.

About the Author

Ron Burgess is a teacher who currently finds himself at the helm of a second grade class, where he's been for the past ten years. Throughout his career, he has sampled several additional jobs such as janitor, shipping clerk, cab driver, truck driver, office clerk, draftsman, engineer, technical writer, technical artist, professional birthday clown, and night club entertainer. Ron is the author of two other books, *Clown Jokes & Walkaround Gags* and *Son of Clown Jokes & Walkaround Gags,* and has also written articles for publications such as *Laugh Makers* and *Clowning Around,* published cartoons in *Good Housekeeping* and *Saturday Evening Post,* and created greeting cards for Gibson, Keep in Touch, and Hallmark.

Ron and his wife Louise-Sandy—married for over 42 years—live in Johnston, Rhode Island, and have five children and seven grandchildren.

Other Great Books from Free Spirit

What Do You Stand For? For Kids
A Guide to Building Character
by Barbara A. Lewis

True stories, inspiring quotations, thought-provoking dilemmas, and activities help elementary school children build positive character traits including caring, fairness, respect, and responsibility. From the best-selling author of *What Do You Stand For? For Teens.* Includes updated resources. For ages 7–12.
$14.95; 172 pp.; softcover; B&W photos and illus.; 7¼" x 9"

A Leader's Guide to What Do You Stand For? For Kids CD-ROM
Eleven easy-to-use lessons reinforce and expand the messages of the student book. Includes additional dilemmas and reproducibles. For teachers, grades 1–6.
$19.95; Macintosh and PC compatible, 5" CD-ROM, reproducible handout masters.

Jump Starters
Quick Classroom Activities That Develop Self-Esteem, Creativity, and Cooperation
by Linda Nason McElherne, M.A.

Make the most of every minute in your classroom by keeping this book close at hand. Features fifty-two themes within five topics: Knowing Myself, Getting to Know Others, Succeeding in School, Life Skills, and Just for Fun. For teachers, grades 3–6.
$21.95; 184 pp.; softcover; illus.; 8½" x 11"

No B.O.!
The Head-to-Toe Book of Hygiene for Preteens
by Marguerite Crump, M.A., M.Ed.

This frank, reassuring, humorous book covers the physical changes of puberty and offers tips on good hygiene from head to toe. Fascinating facts, friendly suggestions, and funny illustrations combine in a lighthearted approach with strong kid appeal. For boys and girls. For ages 9–13.
$12.95; 128 pp.; softcover; illus.; 7" x 9"

Teach to Reach
Over 300 Strategies, Tips, and Helpful Hints for Teachers of All Grades
by Craig Mitchell with Pamela Espeland

A classroom teacher shares hundreds of "tricks of the trade"—ideas to help all teachers sharpen their skills, enhance the learning environment, and make school more enjoyable for everyone. For teachers, all grades.
$9.95; 208 pp.; softcover; 5⅛" x 6"

Growing Good Kids
28 Activities to Enhance Self-Awareness, Compassion, and Leadership
by Deb Delisle and Jim Delisle, Ph.D.

Created by teachers and classroom-tested, these fun and meaningful enrichment activities build children's skills in problem solving, decision making, cooperative learning, divergent thinking, and communication. For grades 3–8.
$21.95; 168 pp.; softcover; illus.; 8½" x 11"

To place an order or to request a free catalog of materials, please write, call, email, or visit our Web site:

Free Spirit Publishing Inc.
217 Fifth Avenue North • Suite 200 • Minneapolis, MN 55401-1299
toll-free 800.735.7323 • local 612.338.2068 • fax 612.337.5050
help4kids@freespirit.com • www.freespirit.com